# BEST-KEPT SECRETS OF JUDAISM

# BEST-KEPT SECRETS OF JUDAISM

## Rabbi Reuven P. Bulka

TARGUM/FELDHEIM

First published 2002
Copyright © 2002 by Rabbi Reuven P. Bulka
ISBN 1-56871-261-8

Published by:
Targum Press, Inc.
22700 W. Eleven Mile Rd.
Southfield, MI 48034
E-mail: targum@netvision.net.il
Fax: 888-298-9992
www.targum.com

Distributed by:
Feldheim Publishers
202 Airport Executive Park
Nanuet, NY 10954

Printed in Israel

*In memory of my beloved wife*

## Naomi (Tzirel Nechamah)

*A rare combination of modesty, dignity,
elegance, faith, dedication, and courage.*

*May this, the last book she proofread,
be an enduring testimony
to her inspired life.*

# Contents

## WITH THE HOME ENVIRONMENT

WITH PEOPLE

## WITH ONESELF

# Foreword

Rabbi Reuven P. Bulka's *Best-Kept Secrets of Judaism* is neither a translation nor an adaptation of the classic *Sefer Chareidim*; rather, it is a distillation from that famous work. And as a distillation, it retains the essence of the original, a profundity masked in measured simple words and a purity that the reader becomes aware of, and possessed of, as he makes his way through the book and is filled with its awe.

At a time of renewed interest in Jewish ethical writings, Rabbi Bulka has produced a work of much originality, which not only opens this hidden world to the uninitiated, to whom it is indeed a "best-kept secret," but is also instructive to the established scholar as to how this ancient wisdom should be presented, so that it can be accessible in our own time.

Rabbi Bulka's work makes an end to the canard fostered by Christianity, and unfortunately absorbed even by some observant Jews, that Judaism is merely an obsession with empty ritual. We learn from this work that ritual, and only ritual, is the great educational tool of God, and we see how ritual transforms us into a great and holy people, a nation of priests.

We come away from this work cognizant of how far we fall from the Torah ideal, and energized to separate ourselves from the mindless and empty culture in which we are mired, while our precious few years on this earth are dissipated in the delusions and illusions of our time.

Rabbi Yechiel T. Perr
Rosh HaYeshivah,
Yeshiva of Far Rockaway

# Acknowledgments

This book is dedicated to the memory of my dear wife, Naomi. Among the many lovely things she did in her full life lived over fifty-five years, she had the patience to read and proof all the books I wrote.

This was the last book of mine that she proofread, and the book is greatly enhanced by her caring touch. My gratitude to her goes far beyond this book, but it surely includes it. May the gains from all who read it be added to the many merits she garnered in her lifetime.

Dr. Aviva Freedman, the dean of Arts and Social Sciences at Carleton University, graciously offered to read the manuscript and went through it with meticulous attention to detail and nuance. The book is greatly improved by her scalpel. My thanks to her for an editing job superbly done.

Blanche Osterer, my secretary, found the time amid

a pressing schedule to help with some crucial preparations for the book. Her ongoing help is most appreciated.

Moshe Dombey at Targum Press has been most helpful with suggestions for making the book a presentable volume. His attention to the project is greatly valued.

D. Liff's cover and design and Suri Brand's proofreading are greatly appreciated. My thanks to them for the caring way they carried out their tasks.

Finally, my deep appreciation to Rabbi Yechiel Perr, *rosh hayeshivah* of Yeshiva of Far Rockaway, for his most generous foreword. Rabbi Perr is a living example of fully integrating the totality of Torah, making him a most admirable and respected leader and teacher.

# Introduction

Does Judaism have secrets? Not in the normal sense of the word *secret*, something shared with a closed group that others are not permitted to know. On the contrary, when it comes to sharing knowledge about Judaism and its practice, we are not allowed to keep secrets.

This does not mean that we must share our knowledge without being aware of who the recipients are. In fact, we are obligated to be constantly aware of whom we are speaking to and whom we are teaching, so that what we wish to convey is received accurately. We must always be sensitive to the possibility that people may not be in a receptive mode, either because of their mood or because of the limits of their knowledge base.

The limits of a person's knowledge base are much in evidence particularly at times when those involved are not even aware of their limitations. For example, in our times mysticism has made it big in the public arena. There are many who would love to study Jewish mysticism, trendy as this subject has become. But it is hardly possible to understand Jewish mysticism if one knows little about the fundamentals of Judaism. It is the equivalent of building the penthouse apartments before firmly setting the foundation. Sharing these secrets with such a person is ill advised.

Another example, perhaps less problematic but certainly an issue, is the rush among some who are understandably trying to make up for lost time to study Talmud without first learning *Chumash*. It can be done, but at a hefty price.

Back to the secrets. We do not keep secrets, but in the pool of knowledge available for us to swim in, there are currents of Judaism that do not get the attention they deserve.

Most everyone can rattle off a list of Jewish precepts and obligations — kashrut, Shabbat, prayer, mezuzah, charity. But there is so much even about these precepts that is not well known. This is a pity, because without this knowledge, our picture of Judaism is bereft of some of its most beautiful and inspirational ingredients. These are what I call "Jewish secrets."

We know of Judaism as a way of life that is founded on faith in God and includes a comprehensive, all-encompassing code of conduct, rules and prescriptions for daily living, special times, and special events.

Because there is so much that one must do, Judaism has often been incorrectly apprehended as concerned only with doing, with little attention paid to "being." This is a distortion and most unfortunate. For those who are discouraged and disillusioned by the apparent lack of soul and feeling within Judaism, this is most tragic.

The true nature of Judaism, its heart and soul, will become more evident in this exploration of authentic Judaism as it was always intended but, for reasons that defy explanation, have been kept secret from too many and for too long.

Judaism, as will become clear, is very much "being" oriented. If we are doing mitzvot, Torah commandments, without being "in" what we are doing, without genuinely and profoundly integrating what we do into our being, we are missing the basic thrust of the Torah, which is to shape us as people (*Midrash Rabbah*, *Vayikra* 13:3). We can hardly be shaped if our deeds are disconnected from who we are and are nothing more than rote exercises bereft of meaning.

Additionally, there are obligations that specifically address the "being" aspect, obligations that are not appreciated as Judaic norms as definitively as they should be.

The main source for all these secrets is itself somewhat of a secret, a seminal work cataloguing Jewish obligations according to the body parts — precepts corresponding with the heart, the eyes, the ears, the nose, the feet — a unique way of bringing Judaism to life.

This book is called *Sefer Chareidim*, written by Rabbi Elazar Ezkari, a contemporary of Rabbi Yosef Karo and Rabbi Isaac Luria of Safed. The word *chareidim* is quite interesting and meaningful. It is not a political term. It is the plural for *chareid*, which means "one who trembles," who literally is in awe of God and the awesomeness of God's word, the Torah. Today we would speak about such a person as one who takes Judaic responsibility seriously, one who endeavors to comprehend the totality of Judaism, including the secrets. In this volume, we expand upon the many nuggets in *Sefer Chareidim*. We used the 5750 Jerusalem edition for this book.

The focus of this book is to lay out some of the secrets of Judaism — those elements whose existence are not widely known, but which manifest the heart and soul of Judaism. The specific secrets themselves are uncovered as key ingredients of the 613 commandments, what I prefer to call mitzvah obligations. It is from among these that we present the secrets, both of the actual obligations and/or of nuances within the obligations.

As an example, the first obligation I expound upon relates to belief in God. It is no secret that belief in God is central to Judaism. The "secret" lies in what it really means to believe. Suffice to say, without giving away secrets, that this belief is much more than an abstraction or a passive expression.

Many of the 613 obligations subdivide into components that are themselves Torah-based, independent responsibilities. These, too, will form an essential part of this book, as they form an essential part of *Sefer Chareidim* and a vital component of the total mitzvah package.

The Jewish package, God's prescription for how we should live, involves much more than 613 mitzvah obligations. It is a comprehensive and profound expression of God's love for us. There is much room within the parameters of the prescription to manifest uniqueness and individuality, but the prescription itself is an all-embracing guide to life that, it is hoped, will bring out the best in all of us.

A word of caution. You may recognize a so-called secret and say, "That is no secret. I knew it all along." I did my best to present what I perceive to be secrets, elements that are generally not well known. There is an unavoidable ingredient of subjective judgment in making the decision as to what qualifies as a secret. There is also an element of the personal in making decisions about how to subdivide the book. It is likewise impossible to avoid overlap in the categories; but that is to be expected, since there is inherent overlap in many of the mitzvah obligations. To the reader who knew it all along, my apologies.

This volume, then, is designed to share the secrets that are so wonderfully presented by Rabbi Ezkari with a wider audience. Every short discourse in this book deals with a mitzvah obligation of its own. There is no fat. The secrets are packaged around a more contemporary expansion of Rabbi Ezkari's usually terse presentation. Once you learn the secrets, share them with others. These are secrets best unkept and best integrated into our full appreciation of Judaism.

# WITH GOD

# Relating to God

## Belief in God

Belief in God is the foundation of Judaism. All obligations derive from that faith. It is technically possible to fulfill obligations without believing in God, and it is preferable to do so rather than not fulfilling these obligations at all. However, obligations fulfilled bereft of faith are denuded of their ultimate meaning.

The actual obligation is to believe that God is the cause of all existence, that God created everything from absolute nothingness, without any partners. The fundamental credo is expressed thus: "Hear, Israel, the Lord is our God, only the Lord" (*Devarim* 6:4).

What is meant by the notion of believing in God? "That we firmly entrench in our hearts the truth of this belief, so that, if asked, we unhesitatingly state that we believe this with all our heart, with our entire being" (*Sefer Chareidim*, p. 49, no. 2).

It may seem obvious that belief in God needs to envelop our beings, that it must go far beyond lip service. But the obvious still needs to be stated. The idea that belief in God must penetrate to the core of our being means that everything we do must reflect this belief, that everything we say and do is permeated with Godliness. Of course, while the idea is almost self-evident, it is difficult to carry through.

The further obligation to recite the Shema, the affirmation of our faith, twice daily — once by day and once by night (see *Devarim* 6:4) — serves to further assure that we remain actively mindful and aware of God's centrality in our lives day and night (see also *Sefer Chareidim*, pp. 76–77, no. 51).

## Stance toward God

Having posited the foundation of belief, the next stage is to describe the essence of our relationship to God. Is it a relationship of fear? Many translations of the mitzvah in *Devarim* (6:13, 10:20) render the relationship imperative as an obligation to *fear* God. But fear of what? Usually it refers to fear of consequence for not following God's commands.

Fear of consequence is certainly preferable to anarchy, to living without values, to rejecting the Godly ideal. But a relationship of fear, though better than no relationship at all, is certainly not our ideal. The ideal is not fear of God but rather *awe* of God. Awe involves overwhelming, transcending love and respect. "That is the higher sense of the term *yirah*, and it is the true, essential sense" (*Sefer Chareidim*, p. 49, no. 3).

Awe of God cannot be on again and off again. If we are truly in awe, then we are always in awe. Temporary, fleeting, or conditional awe is not awe at all.

Testing God to see if faith and adherence to God's word brings with it adequate recompense is out of bounds and is understandably prohibited (*Devarim* 6:16; *Sefer Chareidim*, p. 103, no. 18). The exception to this is charity, wherein God actually asks to be tested (*Malachi* 3:10). Charitableness brings with it guaranteed recompense, immediate and obvious benefits.

Similarly, the high respect implied by *awe* means that we never express God's Name in vain, only in legitimate need, and with befitting, heartfelt — yes — awe.

## *Love of God*

The obligation to love God (*Devarim* 6:5) is likewise a natural component of belief. Once we comprehend the nature of creation fully, its wonders, intricate wisdom, and majesty, we are ineluctably moved to love God, whose love for us is manifest in creation — a love that calls for our reciprocity, "for our souls being bound up in love of God at all times" (*Sefer Chareidim*, p. 51, no. 5). In such a relationship, the idea that there may be other gods, something that is biblically prohibited (*Sefer Chareidim*, p. 100, no. 1), would never enter one's thoughts.

Since we feel awe and love for God, our behavior will reflect this in the joy and eagerness with which we approach our obligations. We are not afraid of God, we are in love with God, and therefore eager to do what God deems appropriate for us.

The love relationship with God extends even further. Singing to God out of love, immersing in the study of God's words, the Torah, at any and all hours, even the middle of the night, referring to God in endearing terms such as "my Heart" or "my Soul," and spreading this love by inspiring others to love God with all their heart are all components of the love relationship with God (*Sefer Chareidim*, pp. 52–53, nos. 6–9). "Our patriarch Avraham is called 'My beloved' by God" (*Yeshayahu* 41:8) as a result of the many people he brought to Godliness (*Bereishit* 12:5; *Sefer Chareidim*, p. 53, no. 9).

Love of God is more than an abstraction. It involves an emotional yearning for and clinging unto God. And more, it means acquiring the behavior patterns that derive from always being cognizant of God, such as awe, modesty, proper thinking, and perfection of character traits (*Sefer Chareidim*, pp. 100–101, nos. 6–7).

Love of God is more than a nice concept to affirm. Just as affirming love of one's spouse without doing anything beyond the statement of love renders that love suspect, so too affirming love of God but behaving in an un-Godly manner renders the affirmation of love for God as a flawed, even distorted, expression.

Though awe and love of God should always be components of our stance in life, "it is more obligatory to manifest these feelings when engaged in the fulfillment of God's commands to us, the mitzvot — the precepts and prohibitions" (*Sefer Chareidim*, p. 52, no. 5). If we fulfill God's dictates out of awe and love, we then view and express these fulfillments not as a burden but as a privilege; not as something we merely have to do, but as something we profoundly want to do.

It is vital to fully appreciate the implications of this concept. It directly contradicts and invalidates the preposterous yet often cited view that Judaism is only a code of doing, with heart, feeling, and emotion playing no part in observance. The idea of a heartless Judaism is false to the core and absurd in the extreme.

## Test of Faith

What if one's faith in God is challenged? What if a person is faced with having to defy God and Godly commands or else be killed? What then? True love and awe is uncompromising and certainly has no room for any public display that smacks of renunciation of God. Fidelity to God is authentic only if it can withstand the challenges to one's personal well-being, one's very life. Thus, in the Shema, when stating that one should love God with one's "entire being" (*Devarim* 6:4), one should understand this as "full agreement — and be ready, should such a challenge present itself — to strengthen oneself to joyfully give up one's life to sanctify God" (*Sefer Chareidim*, p. 55, no. 16).

## Extensions of Love and Awe of God

Since our love of God involves yearning for and clinging to God, it also means clinging unto the Godly — the sages, who are immersed in the ways of the Torah, immersed not only via study, but also via their deeds. "The purpose of the imperative to associate with, to latch onto, sages is to learn from their ways, to emulate them. This latching on includes marrying into their families, having them as business partners, and finding other ways to link with them" (*Devarim* 11:22; *Sefer Chareidim*, p. 54, no. 11).

The extension of the love and awe of God to the sages — loving and holding the sages in awe — is a natural emanation. The sages are defined as those who not only immerse in the study of God's word; they also live out God's word in their lives by adhering fully to the ethics, morals, and affirmations that are contained in God's word, the Torah.

We bring love and awe of God beyond the abstract and into meaningful reality by embracing the manifestations of the Godly — namely, God's word, the Torah — by embracing those who themselves embrace God's word in study and in deed.

A further extension can be found in the case of the patriarch Avraham. For Avraham, there was an automatic path from monotheism, a belief in the One and only God, to monanthropism, one humankind, who are all children of God and worthy of being cared for lovingly. Avraham's success in spreading the monotheistic ideal was thus connected with his propensity for kindness. His success in attracting people was less related to salesmanship and more to impressing people with how love of God leads to love of humanity.

## Trust, Appreciation, and Gratitude

Our faith carries with it a trust in God. For that reason, we are precluded from running to astrologers to find out about the future (*Devarim* 18:13; *Sefer Chareidim*, p. 58, no. 21). Trust in God is directly linked to appreciation of God's greatness and majesty (*Devarim* 4:39; *Sefer Chareidim*, p. 58, no. 22), as well as an

appreciation of all the kindnesses God bestows on us —
yesterday, today, and tomorrow (*Sefer Chareidim*, p. 58,
no. 23).

The expression of our appreciation occupies a central position in Judaism, both as a reflection of gratitude
and as a tone-setter for the general attitude of apprecia-
tiveness that we need to maintain for God, and for anyone else from whom we benefit in any way. The obligation to recall our exodus from Egypt is that central expression of gratitude. Who knows where we would be
had the Exodus not taken place? We therefore thank
God as if it happened to us (*Shemot* 13:3; *Devarim* 6:23;
*Sefer Chareidim*, pp. 58–59, no. 24).

This remembering "is essentially a matter of the
heart" (*Sefer Chareidim*, p. 59, no. 24), not merely of the
mouth. Saying the words is important, but the key is to
*feel* a profound sense of gratitude to God, a core thank-
fulness that is expressed naturally because it is genuinely
felt.

## After-Meal Thanks

The obligation to recite what is popularly referred
to as "Grace after Meals," but which is more

accurately the "After-Meal Thanks," is well known. It is based on the verse "You shall eat and be satisfied and bless [thank] the Lord your God..." (*Devarim* 8:10).

If we properly appreciate the ultimate Source of our bounty, then saying "thank you" is but a minimal gesture of acknowledgment for the blessing we just enjoyed. Anything less would be a manifestation of ingratitude and, to a certain extent, of arrogance.

Those who do not thank are either too self-absorbed to understand that their good fortune is due to factors beyond themselves, or they arrogantly think that everything achieved was done without outside help. That is obviously inconsistent with our profound conviction that without God's help we are bereft.

True, there are others who play key roles in our success, and they must be thanked appropriately. But once we realize that it is God Who is the Source of all provision, and that it is God to Whom we give ultimate thanks, then this expression of thanks must go beyond perfunctory words. Therefore, "one needs to express the After-Meal Thanks with deliberation, with a raised voice, and with heartfelt joy" (*Sefer Chareidim*, pp. 71–72, no. 12).

One who merely mouths words of thanks by rote

misses the point entirely. Just as when we convey gratitude to mortals it is essential to do so in a way that assures that the message is properly received, so too with the After-Meal Thanks to God. This we do by saying thank you with exuberance and joy.

Anything less is simply a collection of words with very little meaning.

## Prayer

Another essential way of effecting and maintaining a relationship with God is through conversation with God, what we refer to as prayer.

Prayer is more than conversation. It includes praise, affirmation, entreaty, and supplication. Prayer is referred to as "service of the heart," not as service of the lips or the mouth. True, the mouth utters, but it is not prayer if the utterances do not reflect sincerity from the heart. Even though the obligation to serve God wholeheartedly (*Devarim* 13:13) applies to the way we carry out all our responsibilities to God, there is a more specific thrust to this obligation, directed to the "service of the heart," prayer (*Sefer Chareidim*, p. 56, no. 17).

The unique mode of expression that is prayer is distinct from ordinary conversation in that it must reflect our love and awe of God. Otherwise it is ordinary conversation and seriously diminishes, if not destroys, the relationship with God.

For prayer to be genuine, it needs to be heartfelt, to spring forth from the genuineness of one's feelings — feelings of awe, of gratitude, of trust. However, for the biblically mandated prayers, including the basic daily prayers, the Birkat HaMazon (After-Meal Thanks), and the regular blessing recited prior to embarking on Torah study, it is necessary to go beyond mere feelings.

The prayers must be articulated, not just read in the mind. In fact, the words need to be heard by the person who is enunciating. Even the so-called silent Amidah, the collection of blessings that are the central prayer for the morning, afternoon, and evening prayers, is not so silent after all.

It is only silent to the extent that others within the immediate area should not be able to hear the praying. However, the one actually praying must make sure the prayer reaches his own ears (*Sefer Chareidim*, p. 69, nos. 7–9). Otherwise, one has not fulfilled the obligation to pray (ibid., p. 76, no. 50).

In other words, when one prays, one should be able to hear what one is praying. Lip service is not enough. By praying without hearing, the person praying suffers in a number of ways. First, the unheard prayer is likely to be a passive reading of words rather than the emotive cry it is intended to be. Second, the unheard prayer involves only a small part of the person instead of involving the entirety of one's being, as it should.

Finally, hearing what one says serves to reinforce what one is praying for. The words of the prayer resonate inside the brain and heart and are more likely to generate or enhance concentration and intention.

Insisting that we hear our own prayers is another way of saying that when we communicate with God we need to be fully and completely in the conversation — body, mind, and spirit. There is no other way.

A part of prayer and its role in our relatioship with God is the special responsibility to be "respectful, and awe-inspired, when in the Beit HaMikdash, the Holy Sanctuary, or any other designated place of prayer or Torah study" (*Vayikra* 26:2; *Sefer Chareidim*, p. 57, no. 19). Levity and idle chatter are totally inappropriate in these places.

## *The Ultimate Expression of Faith*

The ultimate expression of our faith, enhanced and encouraged by the love and awe of God that is reinforced via affirming our faith and prayer, is to emulate God (*Sefer Chareidim*, pp. 56–57, no. 18). But to "walk in God's ways," as we are commanded (*Devarim* 28:9), seems impossible. How can a mere mortal, overwhelmed by the majesty of God, emulate God?

It cannot mean we must emulate God's omnipresence or omnipotence. That is impossible. It is also impossible to emulate God's compassion and kindness, but it is at least possible in this regard to "walk in God's ways." We can never be as compassionate and kind as God, Who alone is capable of ultimate kindness. However, we can, and must, at least walk on the compassion and kindness track and do our best, within understandable human limitations, to be compassionate and kind with our fellows.

Emulating God is the most eloquent translation of love and awe of God into our daily life. It is also the best evidence that we have integrated our profound appreciation of God in the correct manner. Religiosity without an embracing approach to fellow human beings is "sac-religiosity," a distortion of everything holy — effectively a renunciation of God.

## Remembering How We Angered God

Among the things we would rather forget are the times we did not live up to our obligations or were irresponsible. Although we must never harbor delusions of perfection, we nevertheless are likely to feel we should not be obliged to highlight our imperfections.

But that is precisely what is asked of us in a most unusual mitzvah obligation: "Remember, do not forget, how you provoked the Lord your God in the desert..." (*Devarim* 9:7). According to some views, this is a mitzvah obligation for the generations, far removed from the generation that actually provoked God (*Sefer Chareidim*, p. 73, no. 22). What is the sense of placing upon later generations such an obligation?

We realize the importance of our collective history and the need to connect to our past and our roots as part of the continuing tradition that is transmitted from generation to generation. By remembering the good and the bad, we establish that the link with the past is a complete connection, not a selective connection — that we are instructed by the bad as much as we are inspired by the good.

In remembering that we provoked God, we also have the opportunity to contemplate what these provocations teach. They teach that God is patient with the people and allows them to get back on track even though they committed a grave sin. God never gives up totally on *klal Yisrael*, and *klal Yisrael* should appreciate this in its full meaning.

The provocations also teach that in spite of the great deliverances God wrought for us, we not only did not fully express the appropriate gratitude; we actually acted openly and brazenly in a way that could, and did, anger God.

In other words, our ancestors were capable of serious ingratitude. This fact should prevent our feeling any smugness in the matter of faith. If that generation, which was considered on an elevated spiritual level, could act this way, then we most certainly may be guilty of gross ingratitude. Therefore, we must remember their insubordinations and constantly check our own faith to make sure it is not in any way tinged with ingratitude.

## *Remembering How We Anger God*

In the words of Rabbi Elazar Ezkari, "if we are commanded to remember that our ancestors provoked God in the desert, how much more is it incumbent upon all of us to remember that we have provoked God" (*Sefer Chareidim*, p. 73, no. 23). The end goal of this remembering is for us to feel a sense of shame for this provocation and consequently to reconnect with God.

There is more to this obligation than the reconnection with God. This remembering is a potent means to strike a balance in our relationship with God.

It is not unusual, when we feel that we have received an unfair shake in life, to question, even to challenge, God with questions such as — what have I done to deserve this?

When this question is posed, often in an emotional outburst rather than in an intellectual, reasoned approach, there is little attention given to the possibility that we are not nearly as careful in the way we behave toward God as we are in the way we want God to behave toward us.

It is crucial that we feel the pain of others who are

living through agonizing times, but it is equally crucial for us to assess the nature of our relationship with God before a crisis situation arises. We need to seriously contemplate how honest we have been in this relationship. Has it been a one-sided, demanding relationship in which all we do is ask, even demand, of God without reciprocating, without living in a Godly manner, as is asked of us?

When we are asked to remember how we provoked God, we are being asked to look at the traffic flow and to make sure it is not a one-way street. Before we ask questions of God, we must ask questions of ourselves. If we do so honestly, it is less likely that we will have questions of a demanding nature for God.

## Understanding Tragedy

When tragedy engulfs a community, there are certain reflex actions that must take place. When there has been a plague, earthquake, flood, drought, or fire, for example, the most immediate reflex action is to save lives, to help rescue as many people as possible as quickly as possible.

That is the most pressing response, but certainly

not the only response. How should the community perceive the tragedy — only as an unfortunate accident or also as an opportunity presented by God?

It is potentially devastating to suggest to a bereft community that there may be more to what happened, that what occurred was more than an accident. Imposing a sense of guilt and shame can trigger negative emotions, and that is not what is intended. Instead, it is important to realize that no one is perfect and that asking individuals, or communities, to introspect in times of tragedy is nothing more than asking them to use the terrible circumstance as an opportunity for betterment.

When a community is beset by trauma or tragedy, it behooves them to entreat God, to plead for relief (*Bemidbar* 10:9), to repent individually and collectively from their straying from the upright path. They should understand that what transpired was no accident (*Sefer Chareidim*, p. 81, no. 19).

We do not know God's ways. We have no idea why some individuals or communities receive such shattering wake-up calls and others do not. The fact that one has received such a wake-up call is not to be interpreted as a sign of inferiority or special guilt. At the same time, the person or community so awakened is urged not to return to its slumber. It should embrace a new beginning, a new dawn.

As people of faith, we firmly believe that whatever God does to and for us is for the ultimate good, even if that ultimate good seems hard to grasp at the moment.

If one dismisses whatever happens as an accident, one has removed God from the picture. Ultimately, even immediately, that is most tragic.

## Accepting God's Judgment

"You shall know in your heart that in the same way that one admonishes one's child, the Lord your God admonishes you" (*Devarim* 8:5). God's admonishments, which we experience as suffering in various degrees of intensity, are similar to the sometimes harsh reactions of parents toward their children when they misbehave.

This verse is intended to put a distinct perspective on suffering, that the suffering shows God's parental concern rather than a desire for vengeance. The analogy to a parent is suggested not merely as an explanation. It says, "You shall know in your heart...." The analogy is thereby transformed into an obligation: whenever tragedy strikes, be it to oneself, or to loved ones, or, in less intense circumstances, when the calamity strikes only one's property, one should acknowledge the righteousness of the Heavenly judgment (*Sefer Chareidim*, pp. 61–62, no. 31).

Admittedly this is not an easy thing to do, but in the context of the loving relationship one forges with God, such acceptance is more likely to ensue.

The ultimate tragedy, death, is surrounded by affirmations of acceptance of the harsh reality. A garment is torn by the immediate relatives of the deceased with a blessing acknowledging God as the "True Judge." The special *Tzidduk HaDin* recited prior to burial explicitly refers to the perfect ways of God, and Kaddish, which those in mourning recite, expresses the hope for the glorification of God's great Name.

All this may be good psychology, but the impetus for these affirmations is the biblical verse making the acceptance of God's judgment a primary obligation. This is a mitzvah of the heart, to feel in one's heart, through the pain, that what happened is justified.

No doubt it is natural to scream out in agony, to ask

why. But there is a huge difference between a plaintive cry of why, a cry out of pain, and a challenge to God that is rooted in a deficient love of God. It is through the very nature of our love for God that the appropriate attitude to tragedy develops.

The biblical charge to love God "*b'chol me'odecha* — with all one's might" (*Devarim* 6:5) is interpreted as loving God no matter what *middah*, measure, God apportions; accepting everything, good and bad, with joy (*Sefer Chareidim*, ad. loc.). Love of God is unconditional, or it is not love at all. When one adds to this mix the understanding that God's inflictions are the interventions of a loving parent, it is easier to accept the anguish.

This brings us back to the previously cited component of the acceptance of God's judgment. This means that one does not dismiss one's troubles as accidents, that God had nothing to do with them. A loving God does not allow accidents and assuredly intended what transpired.

Though one can never know the ultimate meaning of God's actions, the person affected should use the opportunity of the tragedy to examine his deeds, to see whether anything he did might have precipitated the tragedy.

We know that drunk driving can lead to fatal accidents. We can see the direct line of cause and effect. But there is also cause and effect that is hidden from view, unless in the fullness of one's heart, deeply convinced that God acts out of love, one sees a possible connection between the events and one's own deficient behavior.

In this process, tragedy is followed by soul-searching and repentance. Taking tragedy as a wake-up call, with all the psychological implications of guilt, is a much more helpful and inspiring tack to take — more helpful than blaming God and more inspiring than dismissing what happened as an unfair intrusion on life.

## *Playing God*

Some people, when contemplating whether to embark on a certain course, will look for signs as the basis for the decision. For example, one is in doubt about whether to go to an event. If, when turning on the ignition, the engine does not start, one interprets this as a sign that one should not go.

This type of decision-making is prohibited (*Vayikra* 19:26; *Sefer Chareidim*, p. 114, no. 50). Either there is good reason to go or there is not. Looking for signs as the basis for the decision is wrong.

Similarly, one is prohibited from making decisions on the basis of some anticipated reaction, deciding to marry the first person one meets who will be chewing gum, for example, or the first person who offers a seat on a crowded bus (*Sefer Chareidim*, p. 114, no. 51).

Deciding matters based on artificially created parameters is likewise forbidden; for example, the notion that certain times are good for taking trips (*Sefer Chareidim*, p. 114, no. 53; see also p. 128, nos. 51–52).

Whispering incantations on dangerous creatures to ward off being attacked is another prohibited action (*Devarim* 18:10–11; *Sefer Chareidim*, p. 114, no. 54). Making Torah verses into good-luck charms is included in this category but is even worse because in the process one reduces the Torah from the spiritual to the mundane, from God's word to a good-luck charm (*Sefer Chareidim*, pp. 114–115, no. 55). Additionally, consulting with mediums is absolutely forbidden (*Sefer Chareidim*, p. 115, nos. 56–58).

Underlining all these regulations is the principle that our relationship must be directly with God. The decisions we make should not be based on artificially constructed guideposts that by their very nature deny God by attributing some power to these guideposts. Superstitions, talismen, rabbits' feet, all interfere with our direct relationship with God. Prayer is directed to God, not to a medium. Reliance is placed on God, not on a specially designed ritual.

## Living in God's World

It would be rude and discourteous to take a gift someone has given us and treat it with contempt. Such behavior shows gross ingratitude.

Were we to behave this way regarding the world we live in, it would project gross ingratitude to God. This applies to the great gift of life itself, as well as to life-sustaining creations.

Therefore we are forbidden to destroy any fruit-bearing tree (*Devarim* 20:19). But the caution against waste is not restricted to trees. "One must always be prudent with one's money and not waste even the slightest amount" (*Sefer Chareidim*, p. 127, no. 45).

The preservation of the world God bequeathed to us goes beyond the matter of waste, though the prohibition against waste is a key component of this preservation. Another vital concern is to preserve the world just as God gave it to us. It is perfectly all right to improve the world, but the improvement must operate within specific parameters.

One such parameter is the prohibition of *kelayim* — that we do not conjugally mix different species of animals or fowl (*Vayikra* 19:19; *Sefer Chareidim*, p. 132, no. 76). We are, or at least should be, pleased and comfortable with the species God put into the world. We do not need to improve on creation by creating new types.

This same rule applies to mixing different fruit or vegetable branches or fruit branches with vegetable branches (*Sefer Chareidim*, p. 132, nos. 77–78). The foods God placed in the world are fine, thank you. Our efforts should be directed toward ensuring that the species given to us are planted, nurtured, and harvested as efficiently and caringly as possible. We need not, and should not, create new fruits or vegetables.

A well-known prohibited mixture is that of meat and milk (see, for example, *Shemos* 23:19). Less well known is that this prohibition is directed not only to eating or deriving benefit from the mixture, but even to simply mixing the two together without any thought of eating the concoction (*Sefer Chareidim*, p. 127, no. 46). Just the mixing of the nurturer (milk) with the nurturant (meat) is an intrusion on God's world.

Another arena where maintenance of God's world comes into play is gender. Men are not allowed to wear women's clothing, nor should women wear men's clothing (*Devarim* 22:5; *Sefer Chareidim*, p. 129, nos. 68–69). The regulation also extends beyond dress into behaviors that are uniquely linked to each gender.

This prohibition has great significance for the sanctity of the man-woman relationship, but at the same time relates to the maintenance of God's world — the gender world. This applies, as well, to the regulations with respect to relations between a man and a woman (*Vayikra*, ch. 18; *Sefer Chareidim*, pp. 138–139, nos. 23, 51–55).

On a different level, the spiritual, we must also resist the temptation to improve on God's world as made manifest in the Torah. Adding to the Torah, such as by making tefillin with five compartments rather than the prescribed four, or any other "improvement" on the mitzvah prescription, is prohibited (*Sefer Chareidim*, p. 132, nos. 80–81).

Doing less than the mitzvah prescription, such as reducing the tefillin compartments from four to three, is similarly forbidden. But for those who are more spiritually ambitious the latter would have been obvious; the former, less so. They may have believed that in adding to what God has transmitted they are doing a good thing.

But that is emphatically not true. We do not improve upon God's world or God's words by adding to them. While it may not be our intention, by adding we are saying that what God has wrought for us, or instructed us, is not sufficient, that more is needed.

This is insulting, even arrogant. The world presented to us is good, and the Torah presented to us is complete as it is. It is challenging enough to keep all the obligations God has mapped out for us. We do not need to add to them, or to add within them.

There is a subtle but pronounced difference between adding to the prescribed mitzvah obligation and putting our heart and soul into a mitzvah fulfillment to a greater extent than is asked of us. In the one instance, we are trying to outdo God. In the other, we are trying to stretch ourselves within the parameters given by God. Thus, for example, actively looking for ways to help others, seeking out situations rather than merely responding to situations that present themselves, expands our horizons.

The mitzvah remains exactly the same. But how we fulfill it has been escalated to a different level. We can improve on God's world or words, not by changing them, but by enhancing them through our unique dedication and energetic application.

A final issue with respect to living in God's world relates to the world offered us by our history, its travails and its triumphs.

We celebrate in so many ways the triumphal moment of redemption from enslavement in Egypt. We moved from being slaves to collectively embracing our responsibilities at Mount Sinai. From then on, the agenda, broken at times by the fierce intrusions onto our peace and tranquility, has been to move forward, not backward. That is the world that God has set out for us. Therefore, turning back, taking retrograde steps, to make our home in Egypt, is prohibited (*Devarim* 17:16; *Sefer Chareidim*, p. 136, no. 2).

In the world God has designed for us, we must be forward in our focus, appreciative of our redemptive history but determined to grow beyond it, because of it.

# Above and Beyond

## *To Be Holy*

To place an obligation upon anyone to be holy is a tall order. Yet that is precisely what the Torah asks of us (*Vayikra* 19:2). What exactly does this mean? Is it really achievable?

*Sefer Chareidim* clarifies the meaning of this directive: "One should not say, 'I have abstained from all the forbidden foods and that is enough for me, and among that which is forbidden, I will be of the drunkards and the gluttons who eat meat,' so that all that person's days are like festivals and one chases single-mindedly after the delights of the world. Therefore it is written, 'You shall sanctify yourself'" (*Vayikra* 19:2; *Sefer Chareidim*, p. 99, no. 13).

What pertains to drink applies likewise to gross overeating, vulgar speech, and licentiousness within marriage. In other words, being holy refers to the manner in which we behave with respect to those things that are permitted.

Another related obligation in this regard is to avoid following the narcissistic crowd of gluttonous and drunken idolaters (*Vayikra* 20:23; *Sefer Chareidim*, p. 120, no. 29), whose agenda is far removed from God and holiness.

To stay holy we must emphasize our distinctiveness from idolaters, even in such seemingly innocuous matters as dress (*Vayikra* 18:3; *Sefer Chareidim*, p. 132, no. 82). We must maintain this distinctiveness in all arenas, in order to stay focused on our responsibilities to God.

This concept of holiness is vital to carrying out our responsibilities as prescribed by God in the Torah. With all the rules and regulations that are spelled out in the Torah, there is much that remains permitted. Within the domain of that which is permitted, one can still be perverse, disgusting, abominable. Once we appreciate that the prescribed guidelines are intended to bring out the best in us, to ennoble our every action, we will then be extra careful not to distort the intent of the Torah.

No matter how much prescription there is, one can always do an end run around the rules and effectively make a mockery of the rules without actually breaking them.

The Jewish elastic clause — to be holy — places on us the direct responsibility to go beyond the exact and exacting details of the law. It requires us to do our best to become what God intended us to be in giving us 613 mitzvos, in telling us what we are to do and what we must avoid.

It is nothing short of extraordinary that it is precisely the behavior that we actualize beyond God's word in the Torah that is accorded the label of being holy. What a wonderful punctuation of the importance that the human ingredient — what we put of ourselves into the obligations placed upon us by God — plays in carrying out God's intentions.

## To Put One's Heart into It

In contemplating the role of emotion in the fulfillment of our sacred responsibilities, it is crucial to appreciate that beyond the specific need to put our heart into every single mitzvah, there is an additional independent duty of the heart.

The biblical charge "Place these words upon your

heart..." (*Devarim* 11:18) refers on one level to the general acceptance of all the mitzvah obligations (*Sefer Chareidim*, p. 66, no. 43). More precisely, the phrase "place these words" means that one resolves in one's heart to fulfill God's mandate (ibid.). This is a daily exercise for one's heart — to undertake the full range of Godly duties with one's entire heart. We must not approach any specific mitzvah as a rote activity or mechanical exercise. We also dare not approach the daily agenda in a perfunctory way.

What exactly does it mean to "resolve in one's heart"? Perhaps it is more accurate to refer to this as resolving *with* the heart, with one's full range of emotions.

This mitzvah, this religious duty, perhaps more than any other, counters the canard that Judaism is nothing more than a collection of things to do and things to avoid doing, devoid of any feeling. It is unfortunate that this most profound mitzvah has been such a secret. Hopefully it will be secret no more.

## To Go the Extra Mile

There is a wonderful legal concept — yes, legal concept — within Judaism, called "*lifnim mishurat hadin*," literally, "within the line of the law." Proverbially this concept refers to going beyond the letter of the law.

If we look at the law as a line dividing the permissible from the forbidden, then the area within the line, that the line defines, is far removed from the forbidden behavior, or from borderline behavior. Inside the line one finds the more noble behavior.

Although one can have little quarrel with those who adhere to all the legal obligations, all the spelled-out Judaic responsibilities, there is more to Judaism than the legalities, the legislated "must dos" and "must not dos."

Funny as it may sound, there is a legal requirement to go beyond the legalities, to literally travel inside the line of the law (*Shemot* 18:20; *Sefer Chareidim*, p. 88, no. 33).

Why would the very law say that the law itself is not sufficient, that more than the law is required?

There is a profound message in this. The fact that there is a mitzvah obligation to go beyond the law is a clear statement that we must appreciate the law, not as the ultimate, but as the bare minimum of our requirements.

In every fulfillment we are urged to look beyond the

basic responsibility. We are prodded to look at the ways we can put heart and soul into carrying out the obligations and to look for ways we can add our caring, sensitivity, concentration, enthusiasm, and spirit to the actual deed.

Here is an example. We adhere to the requirements for keeping kosher. And through a more complete understanding of the legislation, we can assure not only that we eat what is kosher, but also that we eat in a kosher way, not gluttonously or disrespectfully.

The extra mile, it turns out, is not extra at all. It is an essential part of the Judaic road map.

# The Torah: God's Word

## Torah Study

Torah, God's guide to life, is the great gift from God to us. As such, the study of the Torah is an imperative that should permeate our lives.

One component of this imperative is to learn Torah at every opportunity from those who teach it (*Sefer Chareidim*, p. 69, nos. 1–2). A second component is the obligation to teach the Torah as the prerequisite for being able to observe and preserve the Torah (*Devarim* 5:1; *Sefer Chareidim*, p. 72, no. 14).

The Torah, as God's gift, is so precious and essential that we must seek it out. At the same time, we must not keep this gift to ourselves. We must share the Torah we know.

But the study of Torah is unlike the study of other subjects, however important they may be. Torah is the essence of life, the way to holiness, the way to actualize God's purpose for us. Thus we are charged with the obligation to recite a blessing before embarking on Torah study or teaching (*Devarim* 32:3; *Sefer Chareidim*, p. 72, no. 13).

Reciting the blessing, thanking and acknowledging God for this great gift, serves to set Torah study apart from other studies. It reminds us that this is a sacred endeavor, sacred as life itself, and singled out in sanctity by the obligation to recite a blessing before learning the Torah.

Torah study may be a subject on a report card, but it is not to be equated with other subjects. Torah is the reservoir of spiritual sustenance as transmitted by God. There is no equivalent.

## Responsibility to Remember

Collective memory is important in Judaism. We are asked to remember what happened to our ancestors. The best-known example is the ongoing recollection of the Exodus from Egypt, as demonstrated in the twice-daily recitation of Shema and in the more comprehensive annual retelling that is central to Pesach.

Less well known, but certainly vital to the continuing actualization of our responsibilities, is to remember the central defining event of our history, the revelation at Mount Sinai. Our ancestors were there, and we are enjoined to remember what happened then, never to forget the experience of revelation as reported in the Torah (*Devarim* 4:9–10; *Sefer Chareidim*, p. 101, nos. 8–9).

Another component of remembering, in addition to the experience of revelation, involves the contents of revelation. We are warned never to forget anything from the Torah that we have studied (*Sefer Chareidim*, p. 101, nos. 10–11).

This is a tall order, even a seemingly impossible order. How can anyone be expected to remember everything learned, never to forget anything?

There are different ways one may forget. One may forget due to cognitive limits or impairments, or one may forget as a result of neglect — not reviewing what one has studied or neglecting one's studies entirely. It is this latter type of forgetting that is the object of concern.

If one fully appreciates the overwhelming importance of the Torah, as God's prescription for living a

meaningful life, this appreciation will express itself naturally in the continuing study of that prescription as fundamental, essential knowledge and awareness. One
would not be able to forget the Torah one learned, any
more than one would forget to awaken in the morning
or to eat.

## More Torah Books

The final mitzvah obligation as spelled out in the
Torah is to write a *Sefer Torah*, a Torah Scroll
(*Devarim* 31:19; *Sefer Chareidim*, p. 91, no. 54).

The ostensible purpose for this is to increase the
knowledge pool within the community. There are so
many obligations and responsibilities every member of
the community must live by. To live by them, one needs
to know them. To know them, one needs to study them.
To study them, one needs the text, the Torah.

By obligating everyone to write a Torah, we prolif-
erate the number of Torah scrolls within the community, making the study of the Torah more accessible to
the multitudes.

These days, since the *Sefer Torah* is generally read
only at public gatherings, in the synagogue, for example,

the main essence of the mitzvah involves printing books of the Tanach (Torah, Prophets, and Writings), the Talmud, and commentaries, and acquiring or publishing halachic volumes or other works with Torah content (*Sefer Chareidim*, p. 91, no. 55).

The key purpose in writing a *Sefer Torah* is to facilitate its study and to bring much needed knowledge to the community.

Originally the Torah was all that could be committed to writing. The oral tradition had to remain precisely that: oral. But as the generations became more prone to forget, it was decided that in order to preserve the oral tradition, it would be permissible to commit it to writing. Hence we have the written Talmud and its further, ongoing explication via commentaries, all designed to help us better understand the Torah.

In the developing scheme of things, it is now the books that explain the Torah that we are commanded to write or to acquire.

Hopefully my writing this book, and your studying it, will fill the requirements for this culminating mitzvah.

# Shabbat and Festivals

## *The Shabbat Focus*

The obligation to keep Shabbat is a central feature of Judaism. It is assumed that Shabbat is one day a week and its observance is one day a week. However, there is more to Shabbat than Shabbat itself. The essence of the obligation to "remember" and to "preserve" Shabbat is that the belief in God's creation of the world be with us at all times (*Shemot* 20:8; *Devarim* 5:12; *Sefer Chareidim*, p. 62, no. 33, p. 79, no. 2). In other words, the obligation to remember Shabbat is a constant, daily obligation.

Another component of the Shabbat focus relates to how we identify the days of the week. What we refer to as Sunday, Monday, Tuesday, Wednesday, Thursday, Friday should actually be identified as the first day toward Shabbat, the second day toward Shabbat, and so on.

This assures that the remembrance of Shabbat is a functional reality (*Sefer Chareidim*, p. 62, no. 33).

Another dimension of this focus is revealed by our handling the good things in life for Shabbat itself — food, dishes, or clothing. The Shabbat reflex, as a derivative of the Shabbat focus, would have us put away all the best items for use on Shabbat (*Sefer Chareidim*, p. 79, no. 2).

Thus Shabbat is an encompassing notion, and the Shabbat focus must be with us all through the week.

What does this focus on Shabbat mean? Shabbat is the time when, unencumbered by worldly, material pursuits, we can zero in on the sacred in our lives — our Godly obligations, the sacredness of marriage, the holiness of parenting, the importance of continuing to learn and to know.

By making Shabbat a daily focus, we imprint in our consciousness the awareness that this world is not about material gain or lofty status. It is about living our sacred responsibilities as reflected in Shabbat. What we do during the week may help fine-tune the Shabbat, but it is through Shabbat that we gain ultimate meaning and fulfillment.

## *Sanctifying Shabbat*

The seventh day of the week, Shabbat, and the festivals, too, are sacred days. Shabbat is the most sacred of these days.

Even though these days are sacred by themselves, their full realization is achieved by our sanctifying them — by making holy that which is already holy.

How is Shabbat sanctified? By our acceptance of the holiness of the day, by our declaring its holiness. "Remember the day of Shabbat to sanctify it" (*Shemot* 20:8). Shabbat, and the *Yamim Tovim* (festivals), are also sanctified through a statement recited on its eve. This statement is called Kiddush, literally, "sanctification."

These days are ushered in via an embrace of their holiness. But holiness has not only a beginning point; it also has an end point. Sanctity does not dissolve into thin air. It needs to be delineated at both its commencement and its conclusion.

At the front end, these special days are ushered in with the aforementioned Kiddush. At the tail end, Shabbat and the festivals are marked off with the recitation of Havdalah, literally, "separation."

Reciting Havdalah is a basic component of the biblical imperative to remember the Shabbat, an imperative that extends to the *Yamim Tovim* (*Sefer Chareidim*, p. 79, nos. 3, 6–9).

According to this configuration, Shabbat and thes festivals are bookended by entry and exit declarations that lock in these days in their uniqueness. If these days were to be ushered in only, but not ushered out, the likelihood is that they would not be appropriately remembered in their entirety. With no official goodbye, a less formal and premature goodbye would be likely. Adhering resolutely to the entry and exit strategy for these days increases the chances that what is in between will also be suffused with holiness.

Another biblical imperative that drives home the importance of appreciating Shabbat and all other holy days is that we add to the sanctity of these days both at the beginning and the end. In other words, we are to usher in Shabbat and the holy days some minutes earlier than the official start of these days and likewise to extend these days a bit longer at the end (*Vayikra* 23:32; *Sefer Chareidim*, p. 94, no. 9). In so doing, we show that these are days we are glad to embrace, to hold on to, rather than seeing them as burdens to endure.

## Yom Kippur

Fasting on Yom Kippur occupies a central position in Jewish life. Even some whose observance is otherwise minimal fast on that day.

One may quibble with the wisdom of choosing a day of total abstinence as the day to be Jewish, since it reinforces the erroneous equation of Judaism with denial, but the reality is that Yom Kippur has been so designated by many otherwise assimilated Jews.

Less well known than the obligation to fast on Yom Kippur is the obligation to eat and drink on the day before Yom Kippur. One who eats and drinks on the day before Yom Kippur is considered as having fasted also on that day (*Vayikra* 23:32; *Sefer Chareidim*, p. 83, no. 6).

This is a biblical obligation, a component of the very obligation to fast on Yom Kippur itself.

A major reason for this obligation to eat on the day before Yom Kippur is so that we may be better equipped to fast on Yom Kippur itself.

The eating and drinking of the day before Yom Kippur is thus slightly different from the eating and drinking on a Shabbat or festival. The food and drink consumed the day before Yom Kippur should be foods that facilitate fasting, bland foods, for example, since eating salty foods before a fast makes it harder to fast.

This obligation is another proof that Judaism is not into denial as a value in itself. Yes, Yom Kippur is a total twenty-five-hour fast, but even though we must fast, it is preferable that the fast not be an unbearable burden.

What sense does it make to urge everyone to focus on repentance on Yom Kippur if the hunger pangs and intense thirst make dehydration likely and concentration next to impossible?

Fasting on Yom Kippur is not an end in itself. Fasting is rather the necessary means to making possible the true purpose of Yom Kippur: a full day of energetic introspection. This is achieved through nutritious fortification on the day before.

## Rosh Chodesh

It is well known that one of the basic ways to celebrate Shabbat and the festivals is via eating and drinking. The message in this is that Judaism fosters integration of all dimensions of life. We do not, in the pursuit of the spiritual, deny the physical. Instead we ennoble the physical by experiencing it in a sacred, meaningful ambience. In fact, our appreciation of God is magnified when we enjoy all the bounty God has bestowed upon us. In this enjoyment, we must strike the right balance. We dare not go overboard in the physical any more than we go overboard in the spiritual.

When we think of the festivals, we think of Rosh HaShanah, Sukkot, Shemini Atzeret, Pesach, and Shavuot. But that is not a complete list. Included in the list of *mo'adim*, appointed times, is Rosh Chodesh, when we also have a mandate to eat and drink (*Sefer Chareidim*, p. 83, no. 5).

This is somewhat of a surprise, since Rosh Chodesh is not thought of in these terms. But it should be.

What is Rosh Chodesh? It is the beginning of the month, sometimes celebrated for two days, sometimes for one. In the prayer services, the Torah is read, and *mussaf* (additional prayer) is recited.

Rosh Chodesh does not currently receive the attention of the community that Pesach does, for example. But this does not diminish its importance. Rosh Chodesh is vital to the proper observance of the special days in the Jewish calendar.

Rosh Chodesh, as the head of the month, is somewhat like a mini–Rosh HaShanah. It is a time to reflect on the actions of the past month and to make resolutions for the new one.

In addition, it is on the basis of the determination of the precise date of Rosh Chodesh that we can know when the other sacred days fall out. We would not be able to observe Pesach on the fifteenth of the month of Nissan unless we knew when the first of Nissan occurred. Thus Rosh Chodesh is the great facilitator, the basis for everything else that is calendar related.

As the facilitator for all the special occasions, Rosh Chodesh itself is special. As the time to reflect and to resolve to make the coming month better than the previous one, it is a great enhancer.

Rosh Chodesh is the unsung and quiet hero of Jewish affirmation. It needs to be brought back into the mainstream of our consciousness. It should never have left.

# The Sacred

## Tefillin

It is well known that one is obligated to wear tefillin, commonly translated as "phylacteries" (*Devarim* 6:8). The tefillin themselves are leather boxes containing excerpts from the Torah that includes an affirmation of faith in God, acceptance of the commandments, and remembrance of the Exodus. Tefillin are bound to the arm and head via leather straps.

The contents of the tefillin reveal a sense of covenant. Binding the excerpts to the arm and head serves as a covenantal act, reaffirming faith in God and a commitment to living out the essence of what these passages contain.

In this context, one can more fully appreciate the rule that "one is obligated to touch the tefillin all the time that they are being worn in order that one not divert one's thoughts from them even for a moment" (*Sefer Chareidim*, p. 86, no. 20).

Tefillin are not mere clothing. Clothing one may put on and forget about all the time they are being worn. Not so with tefillin. Tefillin are a binding connection to God, a reaffirmation of the covenant. Were one to put on the tefillin and then forget about them, there would be little covenantal implication in their being worn. One can hardly affirm a covenant by engaging in a rote exercise.

Once again we encounter a mitzvah fulfillment that is properly actualized via going beyond the mechanical action, fully embracing it with heart and soul.

## *Mezuzah*

Hanging a mezuzah on each doorpost of a home is a fundamental and well-entrenched Jewish practice. The basis for this mitzvah is the verse "You shall write them upon the doorposts of your homes and your gates" (*Devarim* 6:9).

As an expression of love for this mitzvah, many actually kiss the encasement of the parchment scroll upon entry and exit from the home.

What exactly is the operative dynamic in this action? What should be the thoughts occupying one's mind when contemplating the mezuzah?

"One should always place one's hand on the mezuzah upon entering and leaving the house, and remember thereby that God, may God be blessed, is the Master of the house, and the person, the children, the spouse, and all that is theirs are merely guests, and all their property is God's, and it is God Who protects the person at home and in the field..." (*Sefer Chareidim*, p. 86, no. 21).

There is no magic in the mezuzah, but there is abundant meaning in it. The mezuzah is a catalyst for faith.

It is natural for one who has built or acquired a home, or even one who is renting a place, to feel a sense of pride, ownership, and achievement. But there is always the danger that one might think of one's achievements as the result of a solo effort. In all that we achieve and attain, we must recognize that despite the effort we may have put in, it is through God that all this actually happens.

We are guests — lucky enough to be guests —

thanks to God's kindness. Were we to believe differently, we would be well on the way to an arrogance derived from Godlessness that would impact negatively on how we interact with our family and with the world.

The mitzvah of mezuzah sharpens our focus on the truth about life, on the fact that what we enjoy, starting with, but not restricted to, our home, is a blessing from God.

## To Sanctify Kohanim

Those who attend a minyan are probably aware that the *kohen*, a direct descendant of the tribe of Levi via Aharon HaKohen, brother of Moshe Rabbeinu, is given the first *aliyah* (call to the Torah) when the Torah is read.

Less well known is the reason for this. The *kohen* receives the first *aliyah*, is the first to launch any sacred activity, the first to recite a blessing, the first to speak at a sacred gathering. The *kohen* is catapulted into a position of prominence in the community, a prominence that goes beyond veneration.

The *kohen*'s prominence is rooted in the obligation to literally sanctify the *kohen* (*Vayikra* 21:8). We are obliged "to deal honorably with the *kohen* and to give him precedence in any sacred matter" (*Sefer Chareidim*, p. 75, no. 46).

Why do we treat the *kohen* with such abiding respect? Possibly because the *kohen* of old was uncompromisingly committed to enhancing the welfare of the community.

The *kohanim* concentrated on helping the people with their spiritual needs and addressing their problems through their unique, Godly imbued wisdom. Their lives were dedicated to the community, as its teachers and its inspiration. The *kohanim*, in short, were the quintessential public servants, ready to teach, to bless, to guide, to steer people through crises. No other pursuit was theirs, just service to the community.

If we understand the full extent of the dedication of the *kohanim* to the community, then it follows with the full force of common sense that the community should reciprocate by venerating and sanctifying the people who so ennoble the community. We sanctify the people who bring sanctity and Godly purpose to us. Doing anything less would be fundamental ingratitude.

Even though *kohanim* today may not have such

great dedication to their credit, it is the institution of *kohanim* we sanctify, the *kohanim* of yesteryear who uplifted the community, and the *kohanim* of today who stand ready, when the situation presents itself, to step into the role of their ancestors.

# WITH THE HOME ENVIRONMENT

# Parents and Children: The Matter of Honor

*How to Honor Parents*

The obligation to honor one's parents is one of the better known mitzvot (*Shemot* 20:12). Better known, however, does not always translate into better kept.

As a matter of logic, honoring one's parents should flow quite naturally from the sense of gratitude we owe to them for having brought us into the world. But often something peculiar interferes with the logic. Children may see their parents as impediments to their own full flowering. They may resent being in the shadow of their parents; they may resent the authoritarian way in which they have been and continue to be raised. Some may see their parents with all their warts and decide they are not worthy of being honored. And, in general, constant proximity to parents may lead to bad feelings.

All this, as descriptive as it may be of many a family dynamic, does not justify the child's reluctance to honor his parents. This obligation to honor is unconditional.

So basic is the honor due to parents that cursing a parent and hitting a parent are both considered capital crimes (*Shemot* 21:15, 17; *Sefer Chareidim*, p. 110, nos. 19–20, p. 130, nos. 130–131).

The primary fulfillment of honoring one's parents is in the heart, which makes sense, since God desires that the heart be involved in every obligation (*Sefer Chareidim*, p. 64, no. 36). Once the feeling is right in the heart, the rest follows naturally. Asking that the child love the parent with overwhelming intensity, and that nothing done for the parent feels like a bother or great burden (*Sefer Chareidim*, p. 64, nos. 37–38), is not asking much, since the feeling of the heart actually gives birth to an intense expression of love.

The underpinnings of the imperative to honor parents involve profound feelings. "Children should appreciate their parents as great nobles of the world, which is the main expression of honor. With this attitude, they will most certainly honor the parents in word and in deed" (*Sefer Chareidim*, p. 63, no. 35).

To suggest that children see their parents as majestic and lofty may seem extreme, but it conveys the notion that in the child's world the parents should be revered.

One component of honoring parents involves speaking to them in soft tones, in respectful tones, as if speaking to majesty (*Sefer Chareidim*, p. 70, nos. 1–2).

Our desire to honor our parents is likewise evident when, upon being requested by the parent to do something for them, we rush to do so eagerly and energetically (*Sefer Chareidim*, p. 95, nos. 1–2).

The obligation to honor parents involves one surprising gesture. Children are obligated to feed their parents, to help them drink, to dress them and escort them where they need to go (ibid., based on *Kiddushin* 31b).

All this sounds surprising, since usually the reverse is true; parents normally dress and feed their children and chauffeur them wherever they need to go. Why is all this reversed?

Essentially the reversal takes place as the parent gets

older and slowly becomes the dependent one. A parent
is not honored if left alone at this stage, to fall for lack of
support, to be unkempt for lack of care. There is no
honor for the parent who is left to wander with bits of
the day's breakfast and lunch staining the shirt or
blouse. When the roles of life are reversed, we are asked
to do for our parents what our parents did for us when
we were unable to care for ourselves.

But what we do with our parents when they get
older and how we do it is to a large extent related to how
we translate into reality the fundamental obligation to
love our parents. When that love is, at the outset, as
strong as it should be, the chances are much better that
this will be reflected in the way the parents are cared for
by the children in their twilight years.

## The Extent of Honor

The fifth commandment of the Ten Commandments obligates children to honor their parents
(*Shemot* 20:12). But the commandment itself goes beyond honoring parents.

For example, the obligation to honor parents includes the obligation to honor the parents of the par-

ents. Grandchildren are considered like children, and grandparents are therefore like parents and are to be the recipients of honor like parents (*Sefer Chareidim*, p. 70, nos. 3–10, p. 85, nos. 3–12).

Also, one must honor one's stepmother and stepfather. Stepparents are worthy of honor by virtue of their nexus to the biological parent.

And, since husband and wife, upon marriage, are as one, each one's parents effectively become the parents of the other. Therefore one is obliged to honor one's in-laws as well.

One must understand that the honor at issue is above and beyond the elementary respectfulness that must be accorded to all people — an extra dimension of honor that is specific to parents.

The famous fifth commandment is thus much more than a directive to honor parents. It is a directive for class-action honor. Surprising as this may seem, there is a compelling logic and powerful message in this.

Honor does not exist in a vacuum. One cannot honor just the father and ignore or disrespect the mother. No self-respecting parent feels honored if his or her spouse is not also honored. We understand honor as more than just helping with basic needs. Honor includes creating a climate of harmony and respect so that everyone in the family feels good about being part of the group.

How good can a parent feel if the stepparent is reviled by the children?

Can parents feel honored if they see their own parents, the grandparents, ignored or worse by their children?

True honor is achieved when everyone who is attached to the object of one's honor is likewise honored.

## Standing Up

Standing up is considered an act of deferential respect that is reserved for the people in our lives to whom such respect must be accorded.

We are obliged to stand up to our full height for our parents (*Sefer Chareidim*, p. 95, nos. 1–2). This is a component of the obligation to honor our parents.

This deferential standing up must likewise be done for grandparents, as well as for stepparents.

For a sage who has come within four cubits (about six feet) of where we are, we must also stand up. In this way we "glorify the face of the sage" (*Bemidbar* 19:32; *Sefer Chareidim*, pp. 95–96, nos. 3–4).

If we are obliged to stand for a sage who possesses Torah wisdom, it follows that we should stand for the Torah scroll itself as it passes in our presence (Talmud, *Kiddushin* 33b; *Sefer Chareidim*, p. 96, no. 7). In a congregational setting, everyone assembled stands when the Torah is removed from the ark or is lifted or carried around. But they are less likely to stand when their rabbi walks by. That is inconsistent with the regulations regarding respect as written in the Torah.

The obligation to stand extends to all older people, older being defined as over seventy (*Sefer Chareidim*, p. 96, nos. 5–6). This outward display of respect is intended to reflect an inner feeling of deference. It makes little sense to stand up for them but to ignore what they have to say. We stand in awe and thereby indicate a readiness to learn from these people, from their wisdom and from their experience.

These regulations, if carried out as intended, help to create a community of respectful people who value their parents and elders. In so doing, they assure that people, as they grow older, need not fear becoming irrelevant. The older they get, the more respect they are shown and the more they matter to the community.

Another such obligation involves those who testify in court when they have knowledge of facts that can be of help to others. This testimony must be given standing up (*Devarim* 19:17; *Sefer Chareidim*, p. 96, no. 8). This mitzvah conveys the idea that we should be prepared to "stand up" and defend those who are worthy of our help, a vital part of Jewish expression.

## Transmission

Pesach is the time when families come together to celebrate, perhaps more so than any other time of year. It is the time when parents must fulfill a unique obligation, the obligation to relate the story of the Exodus to their children.

If everyone had fulfilled this responsibility from the time of the actual Exodus, we today would have a vivid picture of what happened then. But the chains of transmission have been broken, and what we relate to our children today is linked to, but at the same time disjointed from, the actual Exodus.

It is presumed by most, and not incorrectly, that the

parental responsibility is to tell the story of the Exodus. This is not incorrect, but it is incomplete.

The full obligation is to relate to our children on the fifteenth of Nissan, the seder night, the essence of the Exodus from Egypt and the wonders wrought for us by our Sovereign Creator (*Shemot* 13:8; *Sefer Chareidim*, p. 80, no. 12).

It is this additional nuance that offers a clue as to the underlying, larger purpose of this retelling of the events of yesteryear. The Exodus is the fulcrum event of Jewish history — God's intervention to redeem us from slavery and oblivion. Our daily faith affirmation includes the commemoration of the Exodus. It establishes that our faith in God is not abstract. We do not believe in an impersonal entity; we believe in God, Who watches over us and assures our survival. The parent, in telling the child about God's wonders, is effectively teaching the child an essential, crucial lesson in faith.

For adults, the purpose of Pesach is the renewal of faith. For children, it is to become imbued with faith as a result of the lesson in faith imparted by the parent.

## Inheritance

When people contemplate how to allocate their estate to their progeny, they rarely think about this in terms of its religious components. But there are Torah laws of inheritance, the most salient of which is the obligation to give a double portion of the inheritance to the firstborn (*Devarim* 21:17). This is one of the famous 613 mitzvah obligations (*Sefer Chareidim*, p. 75, no. 45).

One may give gifts to children during one's lifetime, but inheritance is a different matter. Inheritance addresses the issue of continuity within the family, of perpetuating the values that define the family.

In this regard, the role of the firstborn is unique. It is the firstborn who sets the trend within the family, who leads the way in carrying forward the agenda of the parents. The firstborn acts as somewhat of a bridge between the generations, shoring up the gap that inevitably develops between the older and the younger generation.

In recognition of this, the firstborn is accorded a special acknowledgment, in the form of a double portion, conveying our appreciation to the firstborn for the additional role of buffer between the generations.

In this matter, the issue of deservedness does not enter into the equation. Did this particular firstborn live up to the responsibilities that were expected? We consider this no more for the firstborn than for the parent who is to be honored by the children. A lack of parental merit does not attenuate a child's obligation to honor a parent.

Similarly, the firstborn's title to a double portion is not subject to judgment regarding deservedness. Were this not the case, everyone would find sufficient cause to deny the firstborn's due.

This should not be interpreted by the firstborn as entitlement without responsibility. The fact that the Torah guarantees the firstborn a double portion is to be taken by the firstborn as motivation to earn it.

# Marriage

## Betrothal

Marriage is the culminating ceremony binding together in permanent union the groom and bride who have decided to share a destiny together, who have ascertained that they share common aspirations and are compatible.

If marriage is the culminating moment, are there any stages prior to marriage, or can a couple go directly from having agreed to marry to the actual marriage?

It is a mitzvah obligation to betroth one's bride. "Whoever marries a woman without first betrothing her has failed to fulfill this obligation" (*Devarim* 24:5; *Sefer Chareidim*, p. 98, no. 6).

In previous generations, the time between betrothal and marriage was about one year. Today the wedding ceremony actually combines the betrothal and the marriage and is separated by the reading of the marriage contract known as the *ketubah*. The betrothal part of the ceremony, called the *kiddushin*, is finalized through the groom's giving a ring to the bride.

Why is it necessary to have a betrothal before a marriage? Why can we not go straight to the marriage?

*Kiddushin* literally means "sanctification," much like Kiddush on Shabbat and *Yom Tov*. Shabbat is Shabbat whether or not Kiddush is recited. But reciting Kiddush is crucial — those reciting the Kiddush accept upon themselves the sacred obligations of the day. The obligations would still be there, Kiddush or no Kiddush, but Kiddush firms up the relationship between the individual and Shabbat.

In *kiddushin*, the groom sanctifies and hallows his wife-to-be. It is a process wherein the groom becomes aware that this is a sacred relationship, not a narcissistic exercise.

If one would rush straight into marriage without clearly sanctifying the wife, before going through a process that hallows the union, he would miss a crucial step in assuring the meaningfulness of the union.

## The Marital Sphere

Marriage is the sacred union of a man and woman with the purpose of building together a home dedicated to the promulgation of the values expressed in the Torah. The sanctity of the union is reflected in this common purpose and further reinforced by a unique approach to the conjugal relationship.

First of all, relations is reserved for the marital union. Based on a verse in the Torah (*Devarim* 23:18), it is forbidden to engage in sexual relations without sanctifying the relationship. It is also prohibited without the *ketubah*, which details the obligations undertaken for the marriage and is agreed to in the presence of witnesses who sign to this effect (*Devarim* 23:18; *Sefer Chareidim*, p. 137, no. 3).

Fidelity in marriage is preceded by a host of regulations regarding which relationships are permitted and which are forbidden, and what behaviors are out of bounds, whether or not one is married.

For example, consanguineous relationships are by definition prohibited as a capital breach, no matter whether or not there has been a marital ceremony. This includes relations between siblings, parents and children, and grandparents and grandchildren (*Sefer Chareidim*, pp. 136–137, introduction to ch. 32). Even just being alone in a room with a person to whom one is prohibited is forbidden, aside from the obvious exceptions that are of a consanguineous nature, such as parent or grandparent with a child or siblings with one another (*Sefer Chareidim*, p. 139, no. 25).

Deliberate self-stimulation is a prohibited behavior (*Sefer Chareidim*, p. 138, no. 19). There are other actions that affect the sanctity of sexual activity. These include being enticed by the scent of the perfume of a person one is prohibited to marry, such as a married woman (*Shemot* 20:13; *Sefer Chareidim*, p. 121, no. 1).

Extramarital relations are a serious rupture of the marriage (*Sefer Chareidim*, p. 137, no. 12). In addition, if a couple divorce and the woman remarries and is divorced from her second husband, the first husband may not remarry her (*Devarim* 24:4; *Sefer Chareidim*, p. 137, no. 11). In other words, marital musical chairs as an end run around extramarital affairs is likewise prohibited.

What do all these prohibitions convey? If nothing else, they convey a clear message about the sacred boundaries of sexual relations — they are reserved for a legally sanctioned marriage.

From what is proscribed we learn what is prescribed: the husband and wife, in marriage, are one, so much so that no other relationships are fathomable. Fidelity in its true sense reinforces itself.

## Marital Intimacy

One of the essential components of a viable marriage is intimacy between husband and wife, the mitzvah of *onah*. It should be the sacred expression of oneness, and for that there must be a mutuality of desire, a correlation of moods, a synchronicity of spirit.

There is a danger that if left to this type of mutual arrangement, the experience may fall into the cracks. Relations between husband and wife is too important a matter to be left to chance. Clear lines of responsibility need to be delineated.

The primary responsibility rests on the husband. It is he who must be alert to the moods of his wife, to be receptive to her desire and careful of her nondesire.

The operative principle in this dimension of the marriage is that the husband must "gladden his wife"

(*Devarim* 24:5). There is no gladdening when the husband forces himself upon his wife.

But there is also no gladdening when the husband is oblivious to her desires and yearnings. Therefore the Torah states, "He shall not diminish her conjugal rights," assuming, of course, the full and unambiguous consent of his wife. Even when his wife is pregnant, the husband is obliged to fulfill this precept (*Sefer Chareidim*, p. 98, no. 8).

In other words, this aspect of marriage is an end in itself and not merely the facilitator for having children. The mitzvah obligation to make one's wife happy is a constant and applies at all times and in all circumstances.

Anyone who would separate husband from wife and prevent their conjugal bliss is guilty of a most serious biblical offense (*Devarim* 24:5–6; Sefer Chareidim, p 126, nos. 41–42).

Intimacy in marriage gets special attention, because it is such a delicate and vital component of marriage. But it would be a mistake to think that the husband or wife's responsibility in the marriage is restricted to this area.

The husband, as the one mainly responsible, is

never allowed to provide less than the necessary provision of food and clothing that accrues to his wife (*Shemot* 21:10; *Sefer Chareidim*, p. 133, nos. 90–91). As a loving partner, this should never be an issue. The husband should embrace this responsibility as a welcome opportunity to gladly carry out a joyous task, to tangibly convey a loving sentiment.

The love expressed in the fulfillment of the mitzvah of *onah* not only reflects the love the couple feels for one another, but also increases their love and affection.

## *The First Year*

The responsibilities of a husband and wife to each other become operative immediately upon marriage. According to the Torah, one is obliged to be "clean" — true, free of blame — to the household during the first year (*Devarim* 24:5). This means "the groom must become as one with his wife during the first year and should not leave the city" (*Sefer Chareidim*, p. 97, no. 1).

Marriage is a sacred union that is more than just the mutual fulfillment of needs for the bride and groom. It is the building block for the foundation of a solid community.

When a couple marry and move into a new life together, they must realize that as much as they have strong mutual interests and common values, they are also different, unique individuals.

In married life, each has a sacred responsibility to care for the other. Each one needs to know how the other one functions, what excites the partner, what upsets the partner, how the partner handles the stress of the workweek, Shabbat and *Yom Tov*, and any other occasion.

If one is absent, how can one learn all this vital information? If the groom knows that immediately upon marriage he must be with his beloved for a year, never leaving her alone for a night, he will realize that this legally entrenched responsibility is designed to forge togetherness.

Any bride who receives such uncompromising attention will feel more comfortable in the union. And once the union has been solidified via this year-long intense togetherness, the foundation has been put into place for the marriage to grow and thrive.

But why not let each married couple find their own way and set up their own terms of endearment? Perhaps because parameters such as spending the first year together are necessary, if for no other reason than to convey to the couple that the community has a vital stake in all marriages and that the institution of marriage is larger than the individuals in the marriage. It is not only important to marry; it is also important — in fact, a mitzvah obligation — to assure that the marriage works. One year of concentrated effort should go a long way toward realizing this objective.

The community, too, is part of this marital directive. Anyone who is responsible for separating the bride from the groom for the first year, such as an employer who sends a newly married employee away on a trip, transgresses this biblical obligation (*Sefer Chareidim*, p. 117, no. 2).

The community has a stake in every marriage. It also has a responsibility to each marriage.

# The Dependent

## Giving Joyfully

Helping out those in need is a well-established fundamental of Jewish life. Almost everyone is aware of the obligation to give *tzedakah*, charity, to those who need it.

Less well known, but an essential ingredient of this giving, is how to give. The Torah states that "you must surely open your hand to him [the poor person]" (*Devarim* 15:8).

The literal meaning of this directive seems puzzling. After all, how else can one give charity than by opening one's hand? The directive is therefore to be understood as going beyond the giving. It is understood as the obligation to give the charity "with a good heart and with joy" (*Sefer Chareidim*, p. 87, no. 23).

The open hand is a metaphor for an obvious desire

to give, as opposed to a tightfisted approach, which, though it might yield the same amount of charity, reflects a grudging attitude.

A poor person cannot feel good about being in need. Having to rely on the handouts of others is not a pleasant way to live. It is enough that the poor person feels so bad, so vulnerable, so dependent.

By extending help in a callous, hard-nosed manner, we exacerbate the already raw feelings of the poor person. Whatever kindness is present in such an act of giving is more than neutralized by the negative way it is given.

On the other hand, one who extends the charity joyfully lifts up the spirits of the downtrodden poor. By showing an eagerness to help, and a sincere joy in being able to help, we take the sting out of the poor person's pain in being dependent.

One could go so far as to suggest that the ideal way to extend charity is to show the poor a sense of gratitude that we have been given this opportunity to share. Aside from reflecting the truth about giving, this conveys to the poor a sense that they are needed rather than only being needy.

It may not be enough to make the poor feel good, but it is certainly enough to make the poor feel better.

## Loans

Loans, at least on a personal level, are extended to those in need to tide them over difficult times. We understand that it is nice to give a lifeline via a loan to those in need. We likewise understand that it is proper for the poor or the person in need to pay back the loan as soon as possible.

But in Judaism, lending is more than a commercial transaction. The act of giving a loan is considered a mitzvah, an obligation, not an option (*Shemot* 22:24; *Sefer Chareidim*, p. 87, no. 24). By the same token, the repayment of a loan is also considered a mitzvah obligation (*Devarim* 24:11; *Sefer Chareidim*, p. 87, no. 25).

What is achieved by escalating these ordinary transactions into obligations of biblical proportion?

For the person with means, the fact that extending loans is a mitzvah means that there is no choice. It is something the person of "means" must do. It is a sacred responsibility. God is effectively saying to the potential creditor that this is what he should do with the blessing of plenty that has been bestowed on him: The money you have is not yours. It is a trust granted to you provided that you adhere to the terms of that trust.

Another sacred obligation in the loan process is that the creditor must not be oppressively insistent in seeking the repayment of the loan when the creditor knows that the poor debtor has no means to repay. "It is also forbidden to make oneself visible to the debtor if one knows that the debtor canot repay. Even just passing in front of the debtor is prohibited, lest the debtor think the creditor has come to demand payment and will therefore be anxious" (*Shemot* 22:24; *Sefer Chareidim*, p. 117, no. 76).

Another component in the granting of loans is that taking interest is strictly prohibited. Anyone who is party to the interest, including the creditor, the debtor (*Vayikra* 25:37; *Devarim* 23:20; *Sefer Chareidim*, p. 124, nos. 25–26), a witness to the loan, a guarantor, a lawyer, all transgress this fundamental law (*Shemot* 22:24; *Sefer Chareidim*, p. 117, nos. 77–80).

Interest is a way to profit from doing that which one is obligated to do because one is blessed with the means to do it. Having been blessed by God with the wherewithal to help others, we dare not translate this into an opportunity to make more money.

For the debtor, since repayment is a mitzvah, there must be no laxity about paying back the loan. The poor person has no right to say that since the creditor is rich the money is not needed. Nor can one rationalize nonpayment by thinking that since God obligated the rich to grant the loan, this means that God wants me to have the money. It is as arrogant for the poor to withhold repayment for this reason as it is for the well-to-do to refuse the loan.

So this mitzvah is a two-way street, a well-balanced set of responsibilities.

Upon reflection, it is evident that the refusal of the poor to repay will lead to the poor being refused loans for fear that the loans will go into a deep dark hole. Loans, as a higher form of charity, help bring the haves and the have-nots into a better climate of cooperation, a cooperation that would be destroyed by the noncooperation of the poor.

A poor person who has no intention to repay is considered wicked in arrogating the right to determine who deserves the money. That is in God's province. It is for us to heed God's mandate, for us to grant loans and to repay them and thus keep a very positive cash flow and kindness flow.

## Collateral

There are a number of ways a loan can be guaranteed. For example, responsibility for repayment may be undertaken by a guarantor. Or the debtor can assign property or assets to the creditor.

If the debtor is a poor person, it is quite possible that the collateral will be something very basic and necessary.

What happens when the poor person clearly needs the security given to the creditor? Is the creditor allowed to insist on keeping the security on the basis of the argument that returning it would leave the creditor exposed, with no assurance of repayment, with no guarantee?

The law on this is clear. "One must return the security to the poor person for the time that the poor person needs it" (*Devarim* 24:12–13; *Sefer Chareidim*, p 87, no. 28; p. 125, no. 37).

For example, pillows and blankets must be returned for the night, and daytime utensils must be returned for the day. Taking as security items that are needed to make food is prohibited (*Devarim* 24:6; *Sefer Chareidim*, p. 126, nos. 39–40). Furthermore, no security is exacted from a widow (*Devarim* 24:17; *Sefer Chareidim*, p. 126, no. 38).

This is more than just a rule. It is one of the biblically mandated mitzvah obligations.

The issue is so delicate that taking security should not be done save via the *beit din*, the rabbinic court (*Devarim* 24:10; *Sefer Chareidim*, p 125, no. 34). Confiscation of security by the creditor or a rabbinic court agent is prohibited (*Devarim* 24:11; *Sefer Chareidim*, p. 125, nos. 35–36).

As a mitzvah obligation, this impresses on the creditor the realization that there are more important considerations in life than ensuring security for a loan.

There is risk to the creditor during the time that the security is in the hands of the debtor, but that risk is preferable to the alternative: leaving the poor debtor with no blanket at night.

After all, the purpose of extending loans is to help people in need. What sense is there in helping people in need if one creates even more acute needs? That is less of a help and more of an unfair, perhaps even cruel, imposition.

If we care enough to help, we must care enough to avoid causing any harm. That is a biblical imperative, part of the all-embracing Judaic package.

## Wages

It is considered a matter of elementary decency that an employer pay his employee's wages according to the presumed or agreed-upon schedule. Anything less would be deception, fraud, theft, cruelty, insensitivity, carelessness, or a combination of some or all of these.

In spite of the obvious, the Torah does not leave this to chance. It spells out in clear terms that "On the selfsame day you shall pay the wages..." (*Devarim* 24:15). This is a mitzvah like any other mitzvah obligation (*Sefer Chareidim*, p. 87, no. 26). Failure to comply is strictly prohibited (*Vayikra* 19:13; *Devarim* 24:15; *Sefer Chareidim*, p. 124, nos. 27–28).

Obviously this obligation is not a one-size-fits-all regulation. A day laborer must be paid before the end of the following night, a night laborer before the end of the next day, and a contractor upon completion of the contracted work.

Whatever payment arrangement is made at the outset establishes the parameters of obligation on the employer, be it weekly, biweekly, or monthly.

What changes when we make the payment of wages on time a mitzvah? The mindset of the employer changes. It is not simply "nice" to pay the salary on time; it is a sacred obligation, an unyielding necessity.

Excuses such as problems with cash flow or time constraints are not acceptable. Once God says you must, there are no excuses. You must.

"Must" means scraping and scrounging, turning everything upside down and inside out — legally, of course — to find the means to pay the wages on time. Anything less is a sacrilege.

An additional obligation relates to employment in the food industry, such as plucking grapes or picking apples. The employer must allow employees to partake of the food they are working with. For their part, employees dare not abuse this privilege (*Devarim* 23:25–26; *Sefer Chareidim*, pp. 124–125, nos. 31–32), but the employer cannot expect employees to be surrounded by grapes and not eat some, at the very least to prevent dissipation of energy due to lack of sustenance (*Sefer Chareidim*, p. 90, no. 49).

The employer must always treat workers with surpassing respect, never taking advantage of their vulnerability. A worker is not a slave.

# Man and Animals

## Animals First

To emulate God is no small matter, but that is one of our primary obligations (*Devarim* 28:9). How does one emulate God? By being kind and compassionate (*Shabbat* 133b).

Since God's compassion is extended by God to all of God's creations (see *Tehillim* 145:9), we must behave with compassion toward animals.

A person who has animals is forbidden even to taste food prior to having fed the animals (*Berachot* 40a). Not feeding the animals first is considered as having caused pain to a living creature, which is biblically prohibited. Obviously actively inflicting pain on animals is strictly forbidden.

Eating before feeding animals is certainly not an aggressive act of cruelty, but it is a clear instance of insensitivity to the plight of animals. People can control themselves and can therefore delay eating for a while, as we do when we abstain on fast days and when pressing matters divert us from our normal routine.

Animals cannot control themselves. Those who have animals in their charge need to realize this and act accordingly.

Another mitzvah related to animals is the prohibition against placing inordinate burdens on animals (*Devarim* 22:10; *Sefer Chareidim*, pp. 130–132, no. 75). The biblical prototype is threshing with an ox and donkey together, but the prohibition, according to some views, extends to any work extracted from different types of animals by whatever means. Different animals have different strengths, and the pull of one may cause pain to the other, which is forced to keep up the pace.

Another regulation consistent with this general theme is that one must not muzzle an animal when it is doing work in an arena where its food is found, such as in a hayfield (*Devarim* 25:4; *Sefer Chareidim*, p. 125, no. 33).

To bring an animal into the proximity of food, to get it excited, and then put a muzzle on it so that it cannot eat what it obviously yearns to eat, is cruel. The Torah steps in to prevent this cruelty, no matter what impact this may have on the profits accruing from the food production. Profits are nice, but never at the expense of elementary and, in this case, alimentary decency.

## For the Birds

According to Torah law, when coming upon a nest of birds, the mother and her young, one may not take the mother with her young. The mother bird must be sent away, and only then can the offspring be taken (*Devarim* 22:7).

There is a slight complication in actually carrying out this mitzvah obligation. If one is not permitted to take the mother bird, how can one send it away? In the process of sending it away, one is actually taking it.

To avoid this complication, "when taking the mother bird one should do so with the intention not to acquire it, but rather only for the express purpose of fulfilling the obligation to send it away" (*Sefer Chareidim*, p. 89, no. 42).

Many have mistakenly understood this obligation as expressing sensitivity for the birds and have seen this as a legislation that teaches kindness. But how can the act of sending a mother away from her young be an act of kindness? If anything, this seems to be the opposite of kindness.

The Talmud (*Berachot* 33b) actually condemns those who extol this as a compassionate regulation. Taking the mother from her young falls into another category of concern, preservation of the species. Taking for one's own use the mother bird together with her young is taking away the generator of life and her products. At the very least, if someone wants to enjoy birds, he should not destroy the source that gives birth to those birds. In this way, the bird species is more likely to endure for others to benefit.

Taking a mother with her young is a selfish act and exhibits a callous disregard for species preservation, a callous disregard for posterity. Therefore we are commanded to send away the mother bird.

## Burdens

When you see your friend's animal struggling under a heavy burden, you are obligated to unload the burden, to help your friend alleviate the animal's distress (*Shemot* 23:5; *Sefer Chareidim*, p. 89, no. 43). Failure to do so is a biblical transgression (*Devarim* 22:4; *Sefer Chareidim*, p. 124, no. 29).

When you see your friend trying to put a manageable load on the animal, you are obligated to help place the load (*Devarim* 22:4; *Sefer Chareidim*, p. 89, nos. 45–46), although the person you are helping must be prepared to pay for your efforts and your time.

The priorities set with respect to these two situations are telling. If confronted with two situations, loading and unloading, you should help with unloading first. The loading can wait, but delay in unloading means additional pain for the animal, pain we are obligated to prevent (*Sefer Chareidim*, pp. 89–90, nos. 45–46).

What about human burdens? Does this regulation apply only to animals, or does it extend to people struggling under a burden?

If the rule of helping unload applies to animals, how much more so does it apply to people (*Sefer Chareidim*, p. 89, no. 44). This is likewise a transgression when not fulfilled (*Sefer Chareidim*, p. 124, no. 30).

The mitzvah as spelled out in the Torah only mentions animals. There is no reference to human burdens. The extension of the mitzvah obligation to people is a lesson in apprehending the essence of an obligation.

Often the Torah will specify a responsibility with respect to a particular context, either because it is more common or more problematic or more likely to be overlooked. The legislation that one must not destroy food (*Devarim* 20:19–20), is presented in the context of war, when this type of destruction is more likely to occur. Such destruction, however, is prohibited at all times. Similarly, the regulation against afflicting the widow and orphan (*Shemot* 22:21) applies to anyone, but the orphan and widow are mentioned because they are the most vulnerable and hence the most likely to be afflicted.

Our natural instincts would alert us to the visible pain of a person carrying a heavy load, and we would reflexively run to help. We might not respond as instinctively to animals struggling under their burden, since we might think that is what animals are for, to carry loads. It is to avoid such rationalizations that the legislation is directed to animals — not to exclude people, but to include animals.

There is further legislation with respect to employing people. It is an affront to human dignity to work people excessively hard, to place upon them inordinate

burdens (*Vayikra* 25:46; *Sefer Chareidim*, p. 130, no. 73).
People should be treated with respect, dignity, and consideration.

One should never take advantage of one's position and of the fear an employee may feel. When an employee is fearful, one is cautioned against asking employees to perform additional tasks or errands outside their regular jobs, even if the tasks are presumably easy.

Finally, it should go without saying, but unfortunately needs to be said, hitting someone, whether employee, spouse, or child, is the ultimate demeaning indignity. It is the despicable act of a power-mongering tyrant perpetrated on those living in dread of the fear-monger, and is considered a biblically prohibited action (*Devarim* 25:3; *Sefer Chareidim*, p. 130, no. 72).

There is room for parental discipline, but it is limited room. It is particularly when one is in a position of power that one must be careful not to abuse that power.

## *Fit to Eat*

There are animals that by definition are not considered in the category of permissible food. They are more than not kosher (fit); they are *tamei*, impure, beyond acceptability. These include a wide array of animals, fowl, and fish (*Sefer Chareidim*, pp. 83–84, nos. 12–15, p. 119, nos. 10–16).

The signs for these forbidden types are well known. For animals to be eligible for eating, they must have cloven hoofs and a ruminating stomach to chew their cud. Fish must have fins and scales. The forbidden fowl are singled out by name.

Even among those eligible to be eaten, there is a special process that must be carried out in order for the animal or fowl to be kosher. Carrying out this process, called *shechitah*, is a mitzvah fulfillment (*Devarim* 12:21; *Sefer Chareidim*, p. 84, no. 17).

This ritual preparation must be done by a scholar well versed in all the details of this exacting procedure, a procedure which ensures that the animal or fowl is not subjected to even the most minute amount of avoidable pain, such as might ensue if the knife being used were not free of nicks.

But even after all these procedures have been followed, this does not mean that all hurdles are cleared. There is another general regulation that is not well known: we should refrain from eating when the act of eating is disgusting, even if the food we are eating is kosher (*Vayikra* 11:43; *Sefer Chareidim*, p. 121, no. 31). A crude example of this is to refrain from eating a fish until it has died, even though technically there is no ritual procedure for preparing fish before being eaten. The food God has given to us is a precious gift. This gift deserves to be enjoyed in a respectful way, befitting its source.

Actually, eating is a sacred activity — that is, when the eating is done with the intention of gaining the sustenance and strength needed to serve God. In this regard, the biblical charge to immerse certain metal and glass eating utensils in a ritual bath called a mikveh is quite instructive (*Bemidbar* 31:23; *Sefer Chareidim*, p. 92, no. 61).

Immersing the otherwise kosher utensils in the purifying waters of the mikveh serves to accentuate the potential sanctity of eating as a way to serve God — a truly kosher endeavor.

In short, just because a food is kosher does not mean it is fit to be eaten. If it is not kosher, it surely is not fit. But even if it is kosher, it must be eaten in a kosher way, in a kosher setting, with a kosher appreciation.

# WITH PEOPLE

# Relating to Others

## Loving Your Fellow

The obligation to "love your fellow as you love yourself" (*Vayikra* 19:18) is one of the better known but least understood responsibilities.

It is relatively easy to love everyone in the abstract, but this obligation is more than an abstraction. It is a concrete imperative that must be taken seriously. The Sages considered this mitzvah as subsuming the entire Torah (see *Shabbat* 31b).

A necessary step preceding love is the elimination of hatred for others. Hatred gives birth to so many ills, including evil talk, the desire for bad to befall the hated one, delight in an enemy's downfall. An enemy is defined as anyone to whom one has stopped talking for three days because of harbored animosity (see *Sefer Chareidim*, p. 103, no. 19).

If you love some people but hate others, the nature of the love is deemed deficient. The fact that hatred reigns within one's heart means that the love that is extended is a self-serving love. The presence of hatred means that one judges others based on how they relate to oneself rather than unconditionally accepting all people as they are.

The obligation to love is not an obligation to love those whom we choose to love. It is an obligation to love everyone. Hatred stands in the way of fulfilling this obligation and must be eradicated. We should hate the evil, but not the evildoer, save for the very embodiment of evil that is manifest by certain cruel individuals and groups.

After eliminating hatred, how does one go about fulfilling this responsibility to love? Taken literally, this mitzvah is beyond human capacity. To love everyone as one loves oneself literally means that before we dress and eat in the morning, we must dress and feed the entire world, and all this after having not gone to sleep the previous night without assuring that everyone has a place to sleep. No human being can do this. No one has the time, the strength, or the resources. It is impossible.

What is possible is something less demanding, but quite meaningful. It is to praise others, to respect their property as if it were your own, to desire the honor of your fellow as you desire your own honor, to rejoice in the achievements of others and to empathize with them in their failures, and to always speak in a calm, respectful manner (*Sefer Chareidim*, p. 61, no. 28, quoting Rambam).

These attitudes and behaviors do not cost money, should not dissipate energy, and certainly are not time-consuming. They are doable, but not easy.

Take, for example, the requirement to rejoice in the success of others. We may not like to admit it, but it is difficult to rejoice in the success of others, specially when the others are in direct competition with us. Someone who sees everyone else not as a competitor, but as a partner in improving the world, is functioning on a most exalted level. At that level, we see others' achievements not as a blow to our own ego, but rather as an enhancement of God's world. Since we are all in this endeavor to enhance God's world together, every success of others by definition becomes our own success.

Another doable aspect of "Love your fellow as you love yourself" is to praise others. This requires one to adjust one's mindset to look for the good things in others, to find this good, and then to convey praise to others for the good that is in them.

Like rejoicing in the success of others, this is an obligation that costs nothing but demands much effort. Just as delighting in the success of others is not so easily achieved, so is praising others not so easy.

However, this aspect of the mitzvah addresses a fundamental human need. Besides food, shelter, and clothing, people need to feel they are part of the world, that they are noticed, that they matter, that they are appreciated.

It is nice to feel a part of the world, and even nicer if that feeling is rooted in tangible contributions to the world, so that the feeling is more than an illusion. Since we know how much better we feel when we are acknowledged, it behooves us to acknowledge others and thereby make them feel good. In modern psychological jargon, this may be understood as reinforcing their self-esteem, but the exercise is more profound than good psychology.

Making others feel good by saying complimentary things to them energizes them to be even more worthy of good comments and establishes the character of the person conveying the positive thoughts as a caring, sensitive soul with a healthy focus on the well-being of others.

While the words of the mitzvah, "Love your fellow as you love yourself," are no secret, the true meaning and ramifications of the obligation are not well known and certainly not well entrenched.

## To Love the Stranger

In addition to the more general obligation to love everyone, we are specifically enjoined to "love the stranger who is in our midst."

Who is this stranger? In the Torah this stranger is called a "*ger*," a convert to Judaism.

Thus it would seem to be more accurate to refer to this so-called stranger as a "newcomer" to the community. It seems odd to call one who converts to Judaism a stranger. Newcomer, yes; stranger, no.

But a newcomer to the community, even one who has willingly and lovingly embraced Judaism, may feel like a stranger in the new surroundings, and this is what the Torah wants us to recognize.

Therefore, aside from the more universal command to "love your fellow as you love yourself" (*Vayikra* 19:18), there is an additional charge to "love the stranger" (*Devarim* 10:19). One must show, and feel, an added dimension of love to the *ger* (*Sefer Chareidim*, p. 61, no. 29).

Why single out the newcomer for special love? At first glance this may seem unfair to the established members of the community. But upon further reflection, this imperative is perfectly logical.

Think for a moment about the newcomer. Someone who leaves another faith to join the Jewish community does so, or at least should do so, because of a love for what Judaism represents. Otherwise, why switch?

To say that the newcomer has gone out of the way in embracing Judaism is an understatement. It is a change that requires courage, determination, and a deeply felt faith.

Does it make sense for a community so embraced by a previous stranger to be blasé, lukewarm, or even mildly friendly in return? Surely a person who has exhibited, without obligation, an extraordinary love for the community must be acknowledged with reciprocal love. Anything less would be insensitive.

## *Affliction*

To afflict anyone, to make anyone's life miserable, is obviously wrong. But there are certain individuals within the community who are particularly vulnerable and for whom affliction is an even more serious matter.

Generally the dictate "You shall not afflict your fellow" (*Vayikra* 25:17) is a universal prohibition that specifically forbids the verbal affliction of saying painful things, of speaking harshly (*Sefer Chareidim*, p. 110, no. 25).

Singled out for particular concern are the orphan and the widow (*Shemot* 22:21), whom we are ordered to treat with extra sensitivity (*Sefer Chareidim*, p. 110, nos. 23–24).

What seems like an innocuous remark to ordinary people may be felt by the orphan and the widow as painful, as affliction. The orphan and the widow are vulnerable, and we need to be aware of this vulnerability when we speak to them.

An additional prohibition regarding affliction is directed toward our approach to the convert, the newcomer (*Shemos* 22:20; *Sefer Chareidim*, p. 110, no. 26).

The stranger, the newcomer, has no family ties in the community and thus, in a different way, shares a sense of vulnerability with the widow and orphan. If the stranger encounters harshness in dealing with members of the community, he or she is hard-pressed to find support and comfort in the usual places.

Increased vulnerability creates increased responsibility to be careful and caring in any dealings with the widow, the orphan, and the convert. These people generally are more alone and may feel a profound sense of loneliness.

The extra legislated regulation forbidding any affliction of those who are more sensitive should inspire more than just the avoidance of affliction. Because of their delicate state, it is fitting that we go out of our way to be helpful to the vulnerable, to make them feel, via our deeds and actions, not only that they are not forgotten, but that they are appreciated as full members of the community, to be treated with utmost sensitivity.

## Accepting Rebuke

We know of the mitzvah of circumcision that requires one to remove the foreskin when a male is eight days old. We are less aware of another form of circumcision, this one more all-encompassing since it applies to every male and female adult.

"You shall circumcise the foreskin of your heart" (*Devarim* 10:16). What exactly does this mean? As a metaphor, the removal of the heart's foreskin will soften the heart. It will effectively make a hard-hearted person into a soft-hearted person.

A soft-hearted person is more likely to accept the well-intentioned rebuke of others and will be willing to change for the better as a result of the rebuke. A hard-hearted person will refuse all suggestions for self-improvement.

The biblical exhortation to circumcise the heart's foreskin is thus a directive to accept the admonitions of others (*Sefer Chareidim*, p. 69, nos. 1–2). Ego should never stand in the way of improving our ways, to be better able to live responsibly. We must never be so obstinate that we refuse to heed well-intentioned criticism (*Sefer Chareidim*, p. 104, no. 26).

But it is not enough just to be in a receptive mode. The receiver of rebuke dare not harbor dislike for the person extending the rebuke. On the contrary, the receiver should feel increased love for the rebuker (*Sefer Chareidim*, p. 62, no. 32).

It is not the usual pattern among people to take criticism kindly. Ego often stands in the way, because people take the criticism as a personal affront. But criticism is really a compliment both to the person extending the rebuke and the person receiving it. The person giving the rebuke shows a sense of caring for the other, which is laudatory. And the fact that rebuke is extended underlines a confidence that the person who is the object of the criticism is capable of change.

To soften the heart to become a better person is a mitzvah; it involves being prepared to grow and to appreciate those who help in the process.

## Extending Rebuke

Just as there is an obligation to accept rebuke, so there is a responsibility to extend criticism. The biblical charge regarding this is the exhortation to rebuke one's fellow and not bear a sin because of the other (*Vayikra* 19:17).

There are two distinct areas of rebuke (*Sefer Chareidim*, pp. 74–75, no. 29). One involves someone who harmed either you or a member of your family. Rebuking the person may elicit either an acknowledgment of wrongdoing, which is the first step toward reconciliation, or an explanation of the questionable behavior that puts a better light on the issue.

Whatever the response, it is imperative that you extend the rebuke rather than harbor resentment for the other in your heart. That solves nothing and in the long run exacerbates the situation.

Another area of rebuke concerns those who stray off the path and behave in an unacceptable manner, whether that wrongful behavior is toward others or toward God. In either case, the rebuker must approach the offending person privately and in a calm, soft manner. He needs to make it clear to the receiver that the admonition is being extended for his welfare.

Extending rebuke is more than just a cathartic exercise. The person extending rebuke may take the attitude — Well, at least I got it off my chest. But extending rebuke is not designed for the rebuker to achieve psychological equilibrium. It is designed as a way of creating a truly caring society in which those who see others misbehaving do their best to correct the behavior.

Therefore, if after one try at rebuke the receiver refuses to change, one should try again. The rebuker must try to help the person to change unless and until the other party makes it patently clear that he has no interest in heeding the admonition. Failing that, one must continue to make inroads in the hope of changing the wrongful actions.

That is the key aspect of the admonition, that one's focus is on effecting meaningful change. The approach must be soft and caring, yet persistent.

We dare not embarrass the person being admonished. Our intentions may be noble, but we must not tear the other person down (*Sefer Chareidim*, p. 111, no. 27). The goal is to make things better. That is the ultimate purpose, whatever it takes, short of insult, and however often it takes.

## Proffering Kindness

It is nice to be kind. But can kindness be legislated? Does not a mandatory obligation take the spontaneous edge off kindness?

In truth, there is something quite exciting about spontaneous kindness. But more important than spontaneity is the need for kindness to be permanently, forcefully, uncompromisingly entrenched into our psyches as the legally correct way to be.

Unlegislated kindness leaves too much to chance, to personal whim. Legislated kindness leaves us no choice but to be kind. Once we have no choice but to be kind, we may as well be kind about being kind.

Indeed, the Torah establishes the proffering of kindness as a mitzvah fulfillment (*Shemot* 18:20; *Sefer Chareidim*, p. 88, no. 31). Visiting the sick, burying the dead (see *Sefer Chareidim*, p. 88, no. 32), escorting a guest who is departing on a journey (see *Sefer Chareidim*, p. 96, no. 10), accompanying the deceased to burial (see *Sefer Chareidim*, p. 97, no. 11), all fall under the rubric of bestowing or proffering kindness.

These are all mandatory actions that must be part of our daily behavior. We must fit them into our schedule; we must make sure to fulfill these obligations.

Making kindness a must helps to create a caring society. Whatever hesitations one may harbor concerning mandated kindness are more than compensated for by the realization that making kindness obligatory goes a long way toward assuring that it occupies a primary place on our agenda.

Once we know that we must be kind, the chances that we will be kind increase. Once we start acting kind, we get into the kindness habit. When we see the fruits of the kindness, we are most likely to proceed with even more kindness.

It is vital to appreciate that all this kindness is a fulfillment of the mitzvah obligation to emulate God (*Devarim* 28:9; *Sefer Chareidim*, p. 88, no. 31). It is not for purposes of social acceptance that we are to be kind. Were that the case, we would not be inclined to be kind in instances when no one will be aware of the kindness proffered.

Even when society may not expect us to be kind, such as to one who has not been particularly kind to us, the biblical mandate to be kind still holds. Even when we may not feel like being kind, the responsibility to emulate God, to be Godly in our human pursuits, remains.

Mandating kindness may compromise some of its spontaneity, but the mandate goes a long way toward assuring that kindness is the rule rather than the exception, that it is the basic way of being rather than an extraordinary way of being, and that kindness will prevail even at times and in circumstances when the motivation to be kind is not strong.

## Giving Good Advice

No person is so self-sufficient that he does not need help. Assistance comes in many forms and includes both material and spiritual help. We may not realize it, but the natural extension of friendship to others is essentially a form of help. And often the help given benefits the helper as well as the one being helped.

Perhaps the most common form of help offered is advice, whether in simple matters like matching colors for clothing to more complicated matters such as career choice.

Whether we are licensed to give advice, as a lawyer, a doctor, a social worker, or we offer it merely as a friend, there is one fundamental guideline. That guideline is based on the biblical law "Do not put a stumbling block in front of the blind" (*Vayikra* 19:14). From this verse we derive the warning that one may never give advice to a friend that is not proper for that person (*Sefer Chareidim*, p. 111, no. 32).

Another derivation from this verse is that one cannot render decisions on Jewish law that are inappropriate, that result from giving less than the necessary attention to studying the matter (*Sefer Chareidim*, p. 115, no. 61). The issue here is not the actual advice; it is the rendering of decisions. But it fits under the general heading of counsel proffered, which must be given only after full and complete study of the issue.

Usually, when one approaches someone for advice, there is an implied trust at work, a presumption that the adviser will give sound advice, with no intention to deceive or mislead.

It is obviously impossible to obligate people to give good advice. Sometimes, with the best of intentions, the advice given is not helpful. It is understood that this may happen. Indeed, one who is not prepared to take the inherent risk in taking any advice should not seek it in the first place.

But it is possible to decree that no one should give misleading, inappropriate, or deliberately harmful advice. No one except God will know, but this does not diminish the gravity of the offense.

Advice-giving is a central feature of society. People rely on it. The ones giving advice have a sacred, Godly imbued obligation never to breach this trust.

## Visiting the Sick

Visiting the sick is a well-known obligation, yet the nuances of fulfilling this obligation are not that well known.

Just the idea that visiting the sick is a mitzvah, an obligation, is something to reflect on. Everyone will agree that it is nice to visit the sick, but by making such visits obligatory we are in effect saying that visiting the sick is more than an exercise in social etiquette. It is a religious duty, not only in the primary motivation for the visit but also in terms of what is expected as a result of the visit.

When one perceives that one's fellow is in pain, one should feel the other's pain in one's own heart and therefore pray earnestly to God to have compassion on the one who is in pain. The obligation to visit the sick has not been completely fulfilled if a person does not pray for the sick person (*Sefer Chareidim*, pp. 64–65, no. 39).

There is no doubt that just visiting those who are in distress, who are not well, is a commendable deed. Part of the obligation is the duty to communicate with the person who is not well, to converse with him (*Sefer*

*Chareidim*, pp. 76, no. 47), to hear what the sick person is going through both physically and spiritually.

If in the course of the visit one is able to lift the spirits of the sick person, giving him hope for a better tomorrow, that is particularly worthy of praise. Indeed, the term used for this mitzvah of visiting the sick, *bikur cholim*, seems to convey this notion. *Bikur*, visit, relates to the Hebrew word for "morning," *boker*. A person who is not well sees a dark world, a world with no hope, no light at the end of the dark tunnel. A visit that transmits a sense of sunrise, of morning, of hope, is most welcome.

But that is not enough. If the feeling for the distressed person is genuine, then it is natural to turn to the ultimate Source of hope, morning, and redemption, to God, to entreat God on behalf of the unwell person.

This is how caring is expressed in its most profound form — not as a social endeavor, but as religious intervention. A visit to the sick must be followed by entreaty to God.

Another aspect of this obligation is the exhortation to help the sick person repent (*Sefer Chareidim*, p. 76, no. 48).

This is not the usual intent of those visiting the sick, and it certainly is not appropriate to ram the repentance agenda down the throat of the unwell person. Being sick is not pleasant, and we perform no salutary deed by making the sick person feel even worse, which we are liable to do if we preach to him when he is lying in his sickbed.

However, it is important to keep the possibility of repentance in mind when making the visit. If the conversation, conversation being a fundamental part of the visit, turns to spiritual issues, and the person who is not well raises the matter of missed opportunities or regrets at certain actions, then it is appropriate to gently suggest that this may be a good time to renounce those deeds, to repent of the actions about which the person has expressed regret.

Not being a doctor, the visitor may not be able to heal the physical being, but the visitor can play a vital role in saving the soul, in elevating it toward a better tomorrow in the World to Come.

The *vidui*, the deathbed confession, focuses on this directly, but coming around to it in natural conversation is often more effective and spiritually uplifting.

# Keeping the Peace

## Seeking Peace

Seeking and pursuing peace (see *Tehillim* 34:15) is a sacred obligation, a biblical obligation.

Even in times of war, we are obliged to first make overtures, as expressed in the verse "When you approach a city to wage war upon it, you shall call to it for peace" (*Devarim* 20:10; see *Sefer Chareidim*, p. 78, no. 57).

If in a siege against what is obviously a proclaimed enemy one must offer peace to the other side, it stands to reason that this must be our approach when dealing with others, family or friends, who for whatever reason have become enemies or at least much less friendly.

When a husband accuses his wife of adultery, the Name of God is erased as part of a ritual to effect harmony between them, a procedure described in detail in the Torah (*Bemidbar* 5:11–31). This is God's way of impressing upon us the importance of harmony between people.

In the pursuit of peace, it helps to judge others favorably, to extend the benefit of the doubt, to impute to others good motives rather than evil ones (*Vayikra* 19:15; *Sefer Chareidim*, p. 78, no. 57).

It is no surprise that peace is so important in Jewish tradition. It is somewhat of a surprise that the pursuit of peace is actually defined as an obligation. It is not merely nice to seek and pursue peace; it is obligatory. When confronted with a potentially or already explosive situation, we are obliged to deviate from the usual pattern of justifying ourselves, of blaming the other, of standing firm rather than making what we may feel are "ego-compromising" peace overtures.

On a communal level, peace and harmony are essential. A community working in concert is a community better able to address everyday challenges and to provide for the needs of its members.

Even divisions that derive from having two rabbinic courts in one city, with each fostering different practices, do not promote harmonious functioning. Such division is to be avoided (*Devarim* 14:1; *Sefer Chareidim*, p. 133, no. 88).

We have become accustomed to differences that are

derived from distinct communities being uprooted and coming together in new environs. But we should never become accustomed to groups within communities working at cross-purposes. That does not contribute to communal harmony.

Peace is everywhere in our affirmations. The daily main prayer, no matter whether it is a regular day, Shabbat, or a festival, culminates with the yearning for peace. *Birkat Kohanim*, the priestly blessing, concludes with the request for peace. The Kaddish crescendos with a plea for peace.

With the desire for peace all around us, we can do no less than our bit when peace is challenged in our personal or communal lives.

## Disputes

There are many ways to break up a relationship. If one looks hard enough, one can always find an insult or unwarranted remark made by a friend and make this the basis for ending the friendship.

Then there are outright insults that by any standards are so objectionable that no one would blame a person who has been deeply insulted for ending a friendship with the one who insulted him.

But noble behavior goes beyond doing what is socially accepted and understandable. One of the many fascinating regulations regarding the way we deal with others is that we should not rush into confrontation with those who insult us. Instead, we should be one of those who hear the insult but do not respond (*Shemot* 23:2; *Sefer Chareidim*, p. 111, no. 29).

It takes two to fight. By refraining from responding, one avoids a miniwar.

Additionally, there is a further exhortation concerning fighting itself. It is prohibited to be involved in fights. We are to learn the lesson from Korach and his fight with Moshe Rabbeinu, to avoid fights as Moshe Rabbeinu did (*Bemidbar* 17:5; *Sefer Chareidim*, p. 112, no. 42).

The exception to this rule is a fight against those who deliberately mislead the public and cause them to go astray. In those circumstances passivity is wrong (*Vayikra* 19:17; *Sefer Chareidim*, p. 112, no. 43).

Peace and harmony are central values. The Torah goes beyond describing peace as a nice thing to have, as a desirable feature in a community. It urges people to restrain themselves from getting into fights with those whose behavior is less than proper and who may even deserve a stern response. It also urges people to stay away from fights.

These are mitzvah obligations that form part of the total package and which make the search for peace a religious imperative.

## Remembering Amalek

Some things in life we would like to forget, and some things we want to remember forever. Generally we like to remember good things, much as we prefer good times over mediocre and certainly bad times.

It therefore comes as somewhat of a surprise that we are obligated to constantly remember what Amalek did to us (*Devarim* 25:17, 19; *Sefer Chareidim*, p. 73, no. 21) and never to forget it (*Sefer Chareidim*, p. 101, no. 12).

This obligation is presented together with an explanation of precisely what it is about Amalek that we must remember: they attacked us by surprise when we were weak and vulnerable, just after the Exodus from our long enslavement in Egypt, and the attack was launched against the weakest of the people, the ones who were at the rear (*Devarim* 25:17–18).

Amalek's attack was not only a surprise; it was totally unwarranted, since there was no declared war and the people of Israel had done nothing to provoke Amalek.

Amalek's attack was pure evil, the work of a vicious enemy whose hatred of Israel was a forerunner and, worse, a model for the ugliest displays of anti-Semitic venom that Israel has been subjected to throughout the generations.

But why remember? Is it not better to move on, to look forward rather than backward?

In a perfect world, the answer would be that it is better to forget and to move on. But this is not a perfect world; it is a world in which unbridled hate exists, hate which, if left unchallenged, can consume the perceived enemy and many others in its destructive wake.

Remembering, in this case, means being vigilant, to stand up to evil, to give evil no quarter, and to thereby protect the world from physical destruction and moral corruption.

As long as there are people who remember to hate, we must remember that hate exists and that it must be eliminated.

# Justice and Judgments

## Judging Righteously

Judges are not the only ones who judge. Everyone makes judgments of one type or another. Judgments are made when choosing one's marital partner, when choosing one's friends, when choosing what to buy, what to wear, what to eat.

Judgments are part of daily living, whether or not we realize it. So the charge "Judge your fellow righteously" (Vayikra 19:15) is not only directed at judges, who must be just and righteous when rendering legal decisions. It is also directed at everyone in the community: whenever a person judges others, he should do so righteously.

This means that if another's actions can be interpreted in both a positive and negative way, it is correct to adopt the positive interpretation. We are obliged to judge others righteously, to see the righteousness of what they have done.

This is a heart-related approach (*Sefer Chareidim*, p. 61, no. 30). To be able to honestly judge others righteously demands a basic appreciation of others. Those whom we like we tend to judge favorably. Those whom we dislike we tend to judge less than favorably. The actions involved may be the same, but our attitude to the person involved is what makes the difference.

If a feeling of love for others prevails in the heart, then judging those others favorably is more likely. This is another instance of a mitzvah that gets to the essence of who we are and what we feel.

Judging others favorably applies as well to those everyday situations when we may tend to blame others, such as when something in the house goes missing. Instead of pointing the finger at others, instead of blaming someone else, we are told to judge them all righteously. If something is misplaced, look inward rather than outward.

So much ill will is prevented by taking this approach, by not making unwarranted judgments and instead always thinking the best of others.

Similarly, we should not accept the evil we hear about others (based on *Shemot* 23:1). This exhortation, however, has limitations. When the information transmitted has serious implications for saving life, then we should not be so naive as to totally ignore the warning.

For example, "if others tell you that someone wants to kill you or harm you, you should be wary and take precautions. Likewise, if they say that someone wants to kill or harm someone else, you should tell the potential victim that he is in danger" (*Sefer Chareidim*, p. 104, no. 24). As much as we are urged to judge others in the scale of merit, this should not blur the reality that there are times when we must be careful first.

It may turn out that the information about someone being a potential killer is unfounded, and one may then feel bad about having taken measures to prevent a killing or about having warned others about the possible lurking dangers. For that, there is time to apologize. But there is scant opportunity to undo life-destroying damage once perpetrated.

We must take precautions even when we do not necessarily believe everything we have heard. We can be careful in order to save life and save the other's reputation as well.

## Equality in Justice

Judges are directed to "judge righteously" (*Vayikra* 19:15). The immediate question on this directive is, why not tell the judges to judge truthfully or carefully or scrupulously? Why righteously?

The admonition to judge righteously is understood as a charge to the judges to equate the litigants. One litigant should not stand while the other is allowed to sit; one should not be allowed to relate all that is deemed necessary while the other is instructed to be brief (*Sefer Chareidim*, p. 78, no. 57).

The failure of the judge or judges to treat the people involved in the case equally may not have a direct impact on how the judge or judges will reach a verdict. This is certainly not as repulsive a judicial indiscretion as taking a bribe. But it is an indiscretion. And it may pervert, if not justice itself, at least the perception of justice.

A claimant may see that the other person is being treated with more consideration. The other person is not asked to stand; the other person is not asked to shorten his presentation.

One cannot blame a person who, experiencing such apparent judicial favoritism, reaches the conclusion that the judge likes the other side more and therefore will most likely side with that party in the case. The claimant may then argue to himself — Why squander anymore of my time and energy on this case? It is a waste of precious time and effort.

As a result, the claimant may present only a half-hearted and incomplete version of the case to the judge, who, in turn, based on this compromised presentation, will rule in favor of the other side.

Technically the judge has done nothing unethical. But in not treating the parties equally the judge has become vulnerable to receiving an imbalanced and incomplete set of arguments. Based on the arguments presented, the decision may be correct, but if given a more complete set of arguments, the judge might have ruled differently.

The deficiency here is that the judge did not conduct the case with righteousness, treating everyone equally. Judges must beware of how they treat the parties, in addition to hearing and analyzing the evidence with care.

This method of judging obviously has implications for how we would judge extralegal situations, people who have become embroiled in nonlegal but serious arguments. Fairness to these parties includes hearing them equally.

## Judicial Fairness

Asserting that judges must be fair is stating the obvious. Insisting that judges not pervert justice is so fundamental as to be beyond argument.

As obvious as this may be, however, it cannot be left to chance. The Torah includes a general, comprehensive prohibition forbidding any perversion of justice (*Vayikra* 19:15; *Sefer Chareidim*, p. 115, no. 63).

Any bribe, even to judge truthfully, is a perversion of justice, even if it does not involve handing over money and is just the extending of a compliment (*Devarim* 16:19; *Sefer Chareidim*, p. 128, no. 49). Justice not only must be done; it must also appear to be done purely.

This having been established, there are situations

when judges may be tempted to deviate from this rule. One such instance is a case involving an orphan or another vulnerable member of society. There may even be public sympathy, but it is still categorically forbidden (*Devarim* 24:17; *Sefer Chareidim*, p. 115, nos. 64–65).

Another instance is a case involving an evil person. A judge may be tempted to think — Since this person is evil, I will judge in favor of the other person. This, too, is prohibited (*Shemot* 23:6; *Sefer Chareidim*, p. 115, no. 66).

In a case squaring off a rich person versus a poor person, the judge may not decide in favor of the poor because the rich are responsible to feed the poor, and in this way the poor will receive an income in a clean way. Nor may the judge decide in favor of the rich and famous on the basis that a verdict against such a person would be embarrassing (*Vayikra* 19:15; *Sefer Chareidim*, p. 116, nos. 67–68).

The law is the law. Any case that is placed before a *beit din* can be ruled on only on the basis of the facts as presented. No favoritism, however emotionally tugging, is acceptable.

The judge who perverts the law to address societal inequity is distorting God's words. In a distinctly negative sense, such a judge plays God, deciding who should get what based on what the judge deems fair, rather than on what the Torah and the facts say is correct.

After the case is decided fairly, a judge may ask the victorious rich person to show compassion, but that can come only after proper adjudication of the case.

Although this legislation is court related, it extends into the many situations when we are called upon to make judgments between friends or relatives. The same guidelines of fairness must prevail. "My child cannot be wrong" or "My spouse is always right" should never be the basis for any decision or action.

## Modesty in the Wrong Place

I f one approaches the matter of offering instruction, including legal direction, with a cavalier attitude, he is displaying unacceptable irresponsibility and arrogance. Telling people what to do without proper expertise is a serious prohibition.

There are those who, because of their awareness of the gravity of misleading others, opt to keep out of the fray and even though they may be highly qualified may desist from rendering judgment even when approached.

As laudable as this hesitancy may be, and as important as the virtues of modesty and humility are, there are times in life when modesty must take a back seat in favor of the community's welfare.

The verse "to instruct the children of Israel" (*Vayikra* 10:11) speaks of the obligation to instruct when one has reached the level of being expert enough to instruct.

To hold back modestly when the community needs to be led, to excuse oneself from making difficult decisions for fear of rendering a mistaken judgment, is wrong (*Sefer Chareidim*, p. 72, no. 20).

It is wise to render judgment with trepidation, since that will likely save the decision maker from snappy, superficial verdicts. But because the community needs decision makers and legal arbitrators, those who are capable but refrain are being derelict.

Ultimately, being modest does not mean putting down one's abilities to such an extent that one is immobilized from being involved in community issues of importance. That is a result of low self-esteem rather than modesty.

One must, if capable, put humility aside — or at least into perspective — and modestly render decisions with trepidation, but also with acceptance of a sacred and inescapable responsibility.

## Withholding Testimony

I t is well accepted that in general we should be helpful to others. Going the extra mile to help others is even greater.

There are many ways we can be helpful, ways that we associate with charity, kindness, compassion, empathy. However, there are ways to help that we may not necessarily think of as obligatory.

A good example of this is a matter that most people may think of as being an extra, but it is really a basic component of interpersonal obligations. It relates to matters of legal import.

If one knows evidence regarding a matter that is being decided in court, it is incumbent to testify and thereby assure that the ruling of the court is based on the full truth (*Vayikra* 5:1; *Sefer Chareidim*, p. 75, no. 31).

There is a tendency to avoid this kindness out of the desire not to get involved. But that is not an option. You may not want to get involved, but by not getting involved, by withholding testimony, you are automatically involved and in a less than salutary manner.

The Torah-based requirement to step up is a clear directive not to turn your back on those whom you may be able to help. This would be compared to standing idly by as your friend's blood is being spilled (*Vayikra* 19:16; *Sefer Chareidim*, p. 117, no. 81).

By making the need to testify a firm obligation, it is removed from the category of "extra" kindness and becomes basic, the essence of kindness.

In this view kindness is not necessarily what society says it is. Kindness is what is so defined in the Torah. As unpleasant as going to court may be, by not going we harm others whose judgment in court will be affected by the silence of potentially helpful witnesses.

It is not enough to care. If we are in a position to help but fail to do so, we are in breach of our fundamental responsibility.

## Legal Tricks

The Name of God is holy and can be uttered only in warranted circumstances. Making an unnecessary blessing, for example, is considered a breach of the prohibition against pronouncing God's Name in vain, a most serious offense (*Shemot* 20:7; *Sefer Chareidim*, p. 108, nos. 7–8)).

Any oath that is unnecessary, whether it is to corroborate an obvious truth or to contradict an obvious truth or to undertake the impossible, is strictly forbidden (*Sefer Chareidim*, pp. 107–108, nos. 1–5, 10, p. 112, no. 45).

Even agreeing to make an oath in court only as a means to intimidate one's adversary, with absolutely no intention of ever making the oath, is prohibited (*Sefer Chareidim*, p. 108, no. 6). One is not permitted to use the oath or its inherent power as a legal trick.

Another possible legal trick relates to an interesting nuance of Jewish law. One who denies having been granted a loan is not biblically obligated to swear by God's Name that this is the truth. According to the Torah, the presumption is that one would not have the gall to entirely deny a kindness such as being granted a loan.

There is another scenario, wherein the alleged debtor agrees that there was a loan and the dispute is about the amount of the loan. In the absence of witnesses, the debtor who admits to only part of the loan but denies the balance must take an oath in a *beit din* that the indebtedness is only as claimed.

Here is where legal trickery can be a factor. Assume that A owes B fifty dollars. For whatever reason B wants to get A into court to make an oath. B therefore claims that A owes not fifty dollars, but a hundred dollars, knowing that A will only admit to fifty dollars, the real amount owed. But since the claim was for a hundred dollars, A must now take an oath that it was really fifty.

B may be doing this because B has another claim against A for which the court would not administer an oath, but now that A is swearing anyway, they would include the other matter in the oath. This is forbidden, since B is forcing A into an oath A is legally not bound to make.

Any involvement in taking God's Name in vain, whether doing it ourselves or tricking others into doing it, is prohibited. God's Name is sacred, and our appreciation of this must at all times be sacred and inviolable.

# Correcting Matters

## *Repentance*

In Judaism there are a wide range of obligations, including those that come as a result of not having done the right thing in the first place. And it is a good thing that there are such obligations, since it is inevitable that sometimes we, as humans, fail to honor our responsibilities properly.

The most general of these obligations is the mitzvah to repent. Repentance is more than a verbal expression of regret. "The main component of repentance is a heart-related fulfillment, that the person fully regret the wrong deed and resolve never to repeat it for the rest of his life" (*Devarim* 30:2; *Sefer Chareidim*, p. 62, no. 34).

This heartfelt feeling needs to be verbalized by the person repenting, not for others to hear, but for the person repenting to hear. The Talmud states that "prayer was established to be uttered in a whisper so that others would not hear as one admits to a sin and explicitly details it" (quoted from the Talmud, *Sotah* 32b, in *Sefer Chareidim*, pp. 73–74, no. 25).

It is really no one else's business to hear your confession. This is strictly between you and God. But those repenting must verbalize to themselves, so that they may actually hear the gravity of their breach and the fullness of their resolve for the future.

In other words, the move away from error needs to involve the entire being in synchronized regret — with heart, intellect, mouth, and ears acting in tandem.

Repentance is a great gift, an opportunity to make amends, to repair the spiritual divide created by the breach. The intent is obviously not to encourage sin so that repentance may take place. The intent is to assure that, having erred, one has the chance to get back on track in living out one's Godly responsibilities.

## Making Amends

When contemplating the obligations and responsibilities the Torah places upon us, we are inclined to think in terms of the things we must do and the things we must avoid.

However, there is more to the full range of obligations than do's and don't's. Consider the aftermath of having done something that is patently wrong. What happens then? There are mitzvah obligations directed at correcting the wrongs that have been perpetrated in situations when such corrective measures are possible.

Thus, those who have robbed, stolen, or overcharged so excessively as to be guilty of oppression must all return their improperly acquired gains (*Vayikra* 5:23; *Sefer Chareidim*, p. 87, no. 29). Similarly, one who has charged interest on a loan must return that money (*Vayikra* 25:36; *Sefer Chareidim*, pp. 87–88, no. 30).

These are mitzvah obligations that can be fulfilled only if a breach had been committed. They are mitzvah obligations one is better off never being in a position to have to carry out. It is far better not to steal than to steal and then engage in the mitzvah obligation of returning what one took.

But ill-gotten gains, contemptible as they are, must not remain in the wrong hands. Permitting the thief to benefit from theft is only compounding the wrong.

More than simply not being allowed, the Torah declares the return of goods acquired via sinful activity to be a mitzvah fulfillment.

Making amends is an essential ingredient in communal life. Since no one is perfect, we assume there will be dents in the walls of propriety. Rather than letting such wrongs become entrenched, the Torah prescribes corrective measures, which help both the victim and the perpetrator. The victim is helped by having the stolen property returned. The perpetrator is helped by being put back on the track of Torah-based responsibility.

It is hoped that this process will reconcile the criminal with the victim — and with God.

## Circumcision

Barring unusual circumstances, when a male child is born, he is circumcised on the eighth day, as prescribed by the Torah (*Vayikra* 12:13). Obviously we cannot place any obligation on an eight-day-old child. The obligation to circumcise rests primarily with the father (*Sefer Chareidim*, p. 98, no. 1). Usually the father delegates a person expert in circumcision, a *mohel*, to act on his behalf to do the circumcision.

However, should the father fail to carry out his responsibility, or if the child has no father, the mitzvah obligation rests on *beit din*, the ecclesiastical court of the community. As guardian of the community's welfare, it is the court's responsibility to circumcise the child (*Bereishit* 17:10; *Sefer Chareidim*, p. 98, no. 2).

If for some reason the child reaches adulthood without having been circumcised, the obligation moves from the father and *beit din* to the child himself (*Bereishit* 17:4; *Sefer Chareidim*, p. 98, no. 3).

Another mitzvah fulfillment associated with circumcision comes as somewhat of a surprise. The *beit din* has the mitzvah obligation to circumcise those who have converted to Judaism (*Sefer Chareidim*, p. 98, no. 3).

We tend to see the circumcision associated with conversion as part of a procedure. The fact that it is more than a procedure, and in reality is a mitzvah, a sacred responsibility, speaks volumes about the fundamental welcoming attitude to converts. We are obligated to extend an official, covenantal welcome to the sincere convert.

Circumcision is referred to as a *brit*, a covenant. It places the Godly imprint on the person; it is really a covenant with all generations. Since the covenant signifies entry into and embrace of Godly obligation, it is incumbent on the entire community — father, rabbinical court, child — to make sure the covenant is finalized.

# Preserving Life

## Lifesaving

If a person sees or hears that someone is in danger, whether he is drowning or being crushed by falling rocks or being chased or conspired against, it is incumbent on the person to help save him. Likewise, a person is obligated to do whatever possible to heal a person who is dangerously ill (*Sefer Chareidim*, p 88, no. 36).

Included in this general lifesaving obligation is the responsibility to redeem those who have been taken captive. Laxity in carrying out this obligation is tantamount to spilling blood.

Also, if you see a person being pursued by someone who is bent on killing him, you must try to save him even if it means killing the pursuer. But such killing is justified only if there is no other means of heading off the impending murder (*Devarim* 25:11–12; *Sefer*

*Chareidim*, pp. 93–94, no. 74).

Aside from the reactive interventions to save, there are preemptive responsibilities. For example, it is appropriate to have volunteers in every city who are ready to jump in and save anyone who is in danger (*Sefer Chareidim*, p. 124, no. 24).

There are times when one is aware that someone is in danger, but intervention is impossible. This may be the case if the dangerous situation is far away and there is no way to get there on time or if one is not well enough physically to do anything.

Even in these instances, one is not exempt from responsibility. The obligation to save a life is so overwhelming that one must hire others to do the lifesaving work if he cannot do it himself (*Vayikra* 19:16; *Sefer Chareidim*, p. 127, no. 48). Lifesaving is such a serious matter that nothing can be allowed to stand in its way.

Elementary as this may seem, translating this into our daily life patterns is not as forthcoming as it should be. For example, if we are aware that our brethren in certain countries are in great peril, there is no excusing our failure to rally to their support. If protest will not help, if entreaty to one's political representative will not help, then at the very least one has no excuse for not praying to God for the redemption of those in captivity.

In other words, there is always something that can be done. The gravity of the offense of doing nothing should be an adequate prod to assure that something will always be done to help.

There is an additional nuance to be derived from this mitzvah obligation. When someone is in danger, anyone and everyone who is aware of the danger must rush to help.

This is not a responsibility that can be sloughed off from one person to another. Everyone carries equal responsibility. Granted that some people, because of the nature of their relationships with authority figures, are in a better position to help. This only increases their responsibility.

Since everyone is responsible, the ugly specter of a group of people watching as someone is being murdered and doing nothing, not even calling the police or emergency service, is unlikely to occur. The reflex reaction when seeing an unfolding murder is not to see what others are doing. It is to do whatever one can to help prevent the tragedy.

So lifesaving, as elementary as it seems, and indeed

is, actually is a much more encompassing and pervading obligation than we may think.

## Good Fences

The Torah instructs us to fence the roofs of our homes (*Devarim* 22:8). Certain roofs are flat enough and accessible enough to be used for a variety of purposes, including setting up a sukkah, relaxing, drying clothing. But a roof without a fence is dangerous. People walking on it may forget they are on a roof and may fall off and be seriously harmed, if not worse.

What pertains to roofs pertains likewise to other dangers, such as manholes that are left uncovered. Whoever creates or owns the danger is legally obligated to assure that no injury is caused by it. A roof must be fenced; a manhole must be covered (*Sefer Chareidim*, pp. 86–87, no. 22). Failure to do so is a transgression (*Devarim* 22:8; *Sefer Chareidim*, p. 133, no. 92), not only the neglect of an obligation.

This is a broad regulation, including as it does the caution against having a rabid dog or a rickety ladder in one's house (*Sefer Chareidim*, p. 133, no. 93) or any other potential hazard.

One may assume that any normal person would be cognizant of all this and would take the proper steps to remove the danger, without being ordered to do so by God. Why was it necessary to put this legislation into the Torah, making it imperative that we fence the roof and cover the manhole? Are we not better off doing this without having to be told, without being ordered?

Admittedly most people would take the appropriate measures without being instructed. But they would do so because they felt it was necessary and fitting. They would not do so because they were obligated.

What is gained by being obligated? Placing a fence on a roof is catapulted beyond being "nice" or "safe" and becomes a religious duty. In this way the notion that it is in the very nature of being religious to be caring and watchful of dangers to others is established. A truly religious person embraces the entire religious package, of which attention to the fate of others is a basic part.

The mitzvah obligations reveal what God wants from us, what it takes to be a truly religious person, a good person. A good roof is at the top of the list.

## Care of Self

There are abundant regulations concerning what foods are permitted and what foods are forbidden. However, the mere fact that a food is permitted does not ensure its acceptability.

A primary consideration in the acceptability of food is its impact on health. "You shall be exceedingly careful regarding your being" (*Devarim* 4:15) is a sweeping imperative adjuring us to take care of ourselves. The words "exceedingly careful" are employed to convey the idea that danger is a more serious matter than ritual prohibition. An item that is not kosher is prohibited, but an item that is dangerous is even more strictly prohibited (*Sefer Chareidim*, p. 120, no. 25).

A forbidden food or drink that accidentally falls into a permitted mixture is neutralized if the mixture is sixty times the amount of the prohibited item. Usually the mixture may then be eaten.

However, a dangerous substance that falls into a mixture does not become neutralized even if the mixture is one thousand times the dangerous substance. The mixture becomes forbidden.

Drinking water that has been exposed must not be

consumed. An animal that has been bitten by a snake, even if prepared properly, may not be eaten.

The care that must be extended includes more subjective considerations, such as foods that are poison to some because of a medical condition, but are acceptable for others. These must be avoided by those for whom they are dangerous.

Then there are actions, activities, and habits that are so obviously dangerous and place one's life in jeopardy that they should be avoided at all costs.

The bottom line is that since life is a precious gift from God, it would be rank ingratitude to do anything less than meticulously care for this great gift — to care in exceeding measures.

That is the ultimate way of saying "thank you."

## Dignity

As human beings created by God, in God's image, it should not be too much to expect that we carry ourselves with the dignity that befits a Godly creation. Nothing we do should ever cast a negative light on God. Nothing we do should ever result in the desecration of God's Name.

Historically there have been countless occasions when the fulfillment of this imperative took on a different and most unwelcome expression. We were called upon to sanctify God's Name by not capitulating to idolatry, or to the designs of others to force us to renounce our faith. Our history is replete with heroic figures who resisted, up to and including the pain of death, rather than compromise one iota of God's Torah.

Sanctifying God in the most trying conditions projects the most profound and unyielding dignity and is a vital mitzvah (*Vayikra* 22:23; *Sefer Chareidim*, p. 55, no. 16). Fortunately, the conditions for this form of the mitzvah are rare for those living in democratic societies. However, we also have ample opportunity in the arena of daily life to sanctify God, as well as to refrain from desecrating God before others.

For all of us, this means never doing anything that will cast a negative light on God and on Judaism. It means that no unethical or immoral behavior can be countenanced.

For sages, the matter goes a step further. Since sages are looked to as role models, they dare not disappoint by being less than exemplary (*Vayikra* 22:32; *Sefer Chareidim*, p. 135, no. 101).

The dignity we project by the uncompromising adherence to God's word under all conditions, be they trial and tribulation, or merely maintaining one's dignity and principles in a less than dignified and principled world, is a sanctification of God, a glorification of God and the Godly, that will hopefully inspire others to follow.

Dignity is also related to other considerations. There is the dignity of how we present ourselves, as governed, for example, by the rule that men should not shave their hair at the temples or shave the corners of their beard (*Vayikra* 19:27; *Sefer Chareidim*, pp. 128–129, nos. 54–58).

Another is the dignity we accord ourselves by the way we take care of ourselves. Concerning this, the Torah prohibits holding in when one has to get rid of bodily wastes (*Vayikra* 11:43; *Sefer Chareidim*, p. 139-140, no. 56-57).

There is also the dignity that we must accord to other human beings, specially at a time when this is most challenging — after they have died. We are obligated to bury the deceased on the day of death and not wait overnight (*Devarim* 21:23; *Sefer Chareidim*, p. 88, no. 32, p. 128, no. 50). The exception to this is when the delay in burial is intended for the deceased's honor, such as waiting for the mourners to arrive.

In order to accord the appropriate dignity to the deceased, we are prohibited from deriving material benefit from the body (*Sefer Chareidim*, p. 120, no. 28). The body must be buried completely intact.

The override to this generally comprehensive regulation concerns the matter of saving life. If the deceased has a body part that can save the life of another person, then the rule of not deriving material benefit from the deceased recedes in order to fulfill the more overriding obligation to save life. But saving the life of another person after one has passed away should really not be considered an indignity. There can never be indignity in the genuine fulfillment of a mitzvah.

## Returning Lost Items

No one will argue with the notion that it is nice to return lost objects to their owner. It is something we would want done for us were we to lose anything.

This makes eminent sense. Yet more than just making sense, returning lost items is a sacred obligation for those who are capable of so doing (*Sefer Chareidim*, p. 87, no. 27).

Since it is a mitzvah, it really does not matter if the person who finds a lost object would not care about the loss were the situation reversed. We do not engage in the return of a lost object on the basis of its being socially appropriate or on the basis of its being something we would want done for us.

We return lost objects because it is a sacred obligation. This means that we must not walk by an item that has obviously been lost, as if it were none of our business. The Torah makes it our business.

Returning lost objects runs a wide gamut. It includes going out of our way to protect items that would be destroyed if we did not take measures to prevent this.

Consider a scenario wherein a person has found a lost ox or sheep. The obligation to return a lost item places upon the finder the responsibility to sustain the lost ox or sheep until the owner claims it.

Or consider a neighbor who has left a chair out in the yard and is not home, when a sudden downpour threatens to ruin the chair. One who sits idly by and lets the chair be destroyed is ignoring the mitzvah obligation to return a lost item, in this case an item that is in danger of being lost by being destroyed, and is thus a serious breach (*Devarim* 22:3; *Sefer Chareidim*, p. 124, no. 23).

There is a view that the mandate for a doctor to heal stems from the obligation to return lost items. In the doctor's case, the lost item is health.

Similarly, if the finder of a lost ox or sheep must maintain the animal until the owner claims it, it stands to reason that if we meet a lost soul, who needs to be taken in to be nurtured and restored to spiritual vigor, that too is a component of the sacred obligation to return lost items (*Sefer Chareidim*, p. 90, no. 53).

What becomes evident in all this is that the imperative to return lost items promotes more than good neighborliness. It promotes a sense of kinship and responsibility that builds and maintains the community.

# WITH ONESELF

# Honesty

## *Telling the Truth*

In the Torah way of life, telling the truth is an important value (*Shemot* 23:7), though not an absolute, uncompromising value. Also, the obligation to tell the truth does not mean that whatever is true we must say. But whatever we say must be true.

This applies not only when our statements have monetary implications. It also applies to our daily speech — that, too, must be honest speech.

There is an idolatrous tinge to dishonesty (*Sefer Chareidim*, p. 74, no. 26). Lies are usually told to cover up or to impress others whose attitude toward us is so important to us that we lie. But by doing so we ignore the fact that God is also listening; we obviously care less about the impression we are making on God.

Lying thus distorts the nature of our relationships,

placing people before God. This distortion is a diminution of God from the position of absolute awe that we must have of God and is therefore a manifestation of idolatry.

Another form of dishonesty, false praise or unwarranted flattery, especially when it is intended to curry favor, manifests the same distorted values — the fear of humans above God, and is roundly condemned (*Sefer Chareidim*, p. 113, no. 48).

Being honest is more than socially appropriate. We are honest because in front of God lying is impossible. However, there are situations when lying is not only permitted, but it is actually a mitzvah fulfillment. In order to establish peace, it is a mitzvah to lie if that is the only way to make peace (Talmud, *Yevamot* 65b), be it between spouses or family members or friends.

Since the value of honesty is rooted in our relationship with God, the parameters of honesty are established by God. If God says it is acceptable, even laudable, to lie for the sake of peace, that peace is of higher value, then that is the ultimate honesty.

## Integrity

When different parts of an entity work well together, we say the system is well integrated. What do we mean when we say that a person has integrity? Usually we mean that the person is honest to the core and always projects, in his every word, his true inner feelings.

It is obligatory for one's mouth and one's heart to be in harmony, so that one says nothing that does not reflect one's true beliefs or ideals or feelings (*Vayikra* 19:36; *Sefer Chareidim*, p. 78, no. 59).

Why would anyone do anything less than say what is in his heart? Usually, but certainly not always, to make a favorable impression. Sometimes the less than honest expression may be the result of a real fear or perceived danger in saying what one would really like to say.

Only mindreaders can know what resides in the deeper recesses of our hearts. Saying things we do not really mean is as difficult to discern as it is wrong to say.

Who will know? Only God. But that is a very big "only." If there is any impression we need to make in life, it is primarily on God. God cannot be fooled. God knows what we really think.

The responsibility to speak the integrated truth, a verbal expression that coincides with the vibrations of the heart, is a social obligation that is deeply rooted in faith.

It is not out of fear of God, but from our awareness of God's omnipresence, that we should never dare to give false impressions. To care more about what others think than about what God knows is a most serious perversion of faith.

On the other hand, this obligation is not to be translated as a call to blurt out everything that resides inside. If — emphasis on if — we speak, it should be the full truth. But there are times when the truth may hurt unnecessarily. That is the time to be silent. This, too, is a mark of integrity, of modesty, of humility, of self-control, of being true to one's higher responsibility to be caring and empathetic.

## Being Up Front

There are times in life when people are at a disadvantage. They are not aware of certain facts or realities that affect decision-making, facts and realities that others with whom they are dealing are fully aware.

For example, the rule is that a loan that has passed over the sabbatical year is automatically canceled unless a special document had been legally arranged concerning the loan. If an unaware debtor approaches an aware creditor following the conclusion of the *shemittah* (sabbatical year) with a desire to repay the loan, the creditor must tell the debtor that there is no legal right to demand payment (*Devarim* 15:2; *Sefer Chareidim*, p. 80, no. 16). If the debtor nevertheless insists on repaying, the creditor may accept.

Another instance concerns a person who was convicted of having killed accidentally with culpability, since there was some measure of negligence. Such a person is sent to exile, to a city of refuge. Were that person to come to a place wherein the people of the city desire to bestow honor upon him, he must tell them that he is a killer and not worthy of honor. Should they nevertheless still insist on honoring him, he may accept (*Devarim* 19:4; *Sefer Chareidim*, p. 80, no. 17).

This regulation applies even in our times, when there is no official city of refuge. It is possible that a person may be driven out of his hometown by a community that is incensed that his negligence caused a death.

The common thread in both these biblically based charges to disclose the law or the facts is that we must never take advantage of the unawareness of others, even if that lack of awareness is a result of ignorance of the law that people usually know or should know.

We must not resort to the often employed responses — You should have known or You should have asked. Life is not a game of trying to outwit and outsmart others. One should be up front about the reality at all times. We must never take advantage of others.

Whatever material profit we may gain from such gamesmanship pales in comparison with the nobility of character that is displayed in being fair.

## Theft

Theft and robbery are forbidden, plain and simple (*Vayikra* 19:13; *Sefer Chareidim*, p. 123, nos. 12–13). But the extent of the prohibition is not so plain and simple.

For example, the victim of a theft is not permitted to steal the item back from the thief, even though this would restore the status quo. There may be justification in one's mind for doing this, but in the process one tastes what it is to be a thief. The prohibition regarding theft is all-encompassing. (*Sefer Chareidim*, p. 123, no. 17).

A more tricky area of theft is what may be best translated as monetary oppression. This concerns over-valuing an item for sale or undervaluing it for purchase. These are instances of monetary oppression and are strictly forbidden (*Vayikra* 25:14; *Sefer Chareidim*, p. 124, nos. 21–22). Taking advantage of others for whatever reason, be it because they are desperate or because they are unaware of the true value, is not an option in the Jewish marketplace. Earning a profit has its limits.

Another form of stealing frequently indulged in but also prohibited is "mind-stealing," commonly referred to as deception. The more extreme instances of mind-stealing, fraudulently dressing up a used item to look new, blowing things up to appear bigger than they are, or hiding a defect in an item are all in the category of theft.

A more subtle form of mind-stealing occurs when one conveys an incorrect impression with deliberate intent to deceive. Classic in this regard is sending an invitation to someone for an event when one knows that the invitee cannot attend and the inviter would not have extended the invitation had he been able to attend. This is mind-stealing in that it conveys a sense of friendship to the invitee that is clearly not real.

Avoiding theft of all types is thus not a simple matter. But by being honest and up front, in a kind manner, one will avoid all these pitfalls.

## Accurate Measures

There is no room for laxity in the sale of items that are purchased via weight or measure, by the pound or by the foot. All the measuring instruments must be accurate. It is the sacred obligation of those who deal in commodities for which measuring utensils are needed that they make sure of the accuracy of the measures rather than rely on the presumption that they are accurate (*Vayikra* 19:36; *Sefer Chareidim*, p. 88, no. 35).

The condemnation of those who deliberately employ false weights and measures is thunderous. This is considered worse than sexual impropriety, and the person committing this type of crime is branded as evil, disgusting, hated, rejected, abominable (*Vayikra* 19:35; *Sefer Chareidim*, p. 134, no. 96).

The extent of the concern about honest weights and measures is reflected in the prohibition forbidding the mere presence of false weights and measures, even if these are not intended for use in transactions. "One is obliged to destroy these false measures so they do not become a snare. One who keeps them violates a prohibition" (*Devarim* 25:13–14; *Sefer Chareidim*, p. 134, no. 97).

There is nothing intrinsically wrong with having an inaccurate measuring bowl, for example, if the bowl is being used as a door stop. Still, the bowl must be destroyed. False measures are too dangerous to keep on hand. One can never be certain that in an emergency they will not be used. One cannot be assured that others, not knowing that these measures are inaccurate, will not use them.

False measures are the moral equivalent of environmental pollutants, with the potential to cause severe damage and immense harm.

# Speech

## *Idle Chatter*

One of the generally accepted behavioral norms in society is to navigate through a social gathering saying the common platitudes and talking about nothing important in a nice manner. As long as the conversation does not degenerate into bad-mouthing and one says nothing harmful or useful, it is considered beyond reproach. In the way of thinking that prevails in society, if no harm has been caused, there is nothing wrong.

But there is a larger issue here that is often neglected. If useful things could have been achieved during this time, then the time spent on inanities is a waste of the most precious gift we have in life, time itself.

The Torah injunction "you shall converse with them..." (*Devarim* 6:7) refers to the responsibility to make our conversation "with them," with the words of the Torah and not in idle chatter (*Sefer Chareidim*, p. 74, no. 27).

It is important to appreciate that what is meant by conversing on Torah matters is not only discussing points of law, or interpretation of text, or discourse. If the conversation centers on how to improve the plight of the poor or the disadvantaged, or how to infuse society with a better sense of morals and ethics, this, too, falls within the broad sense of Torah.

Idle chatter is not necessarily harmful, but it is most often useless and purposeless, and therefore a deviation from the course of meaningfulness that we should always be on. It is not only through doing wrong that we deviate. We can also deviate by failing to actualize what is right, by squandering opportunities to help others and make the world a better place to live in.

The directive to avoid idle chatter pushes us to zero in on the way we handle our time, how we make the most of our opportunities and our speech.

## Bad Talk

It is generally accepted within society that one may speak ill of others, as long as it is the truth. If it is a lie, it is slander and subject to legal action. But otherwise the law has no power to stop such negative talk.

Not so in Jewish law. Bad talk is prohibited precisely when it is the truth (*Shemot* 23:1; *Sefer Chareidim*, p. 111, no. 33). Also prohibited is reporting the negative remarks expressed by others to the subject of those remarks (*Vayikra* 19:16; *Sefer Chareidim*, p. 112, no. 38). When the bad speech is also untrue, it comes under the heading of slander and is obviously forbidden (*Sefer Chareidim*, p. 111, nos. 35–36).

The tongue is a powerful organ. Words can destroy people; words can uplift people. We are warned that talking badly about others should not be a way that we exercise our tongues. Speech has been given to us as a gift, in order to teach, to inspire, to raise up spirits, not to destroy others.

If we do not have anything good to say of others, we should say nothing. Talking ill of others is destructive to the person doing the talking, those doing the listening, and the person being talked about.

The extent of this is felt in the legislation regarding murder. "You shall not murder" (*Shemot* 20:13) is a well-known prohibition. Less well known is the following: causing another's face to turn pale because you insulted him, causing the blood to drain from his face, is like committing murder (*Sefer Chareidim*, p. 122, no. 9).

This is not hyperbole. It is an essential law that must govern our talk.

Another type of bad talk that is strictly prohibited is foul language, speech that may not hurt others but is by its very nature degrading. Off-color speech is out of bounds, no matter how accepted such speech may be in general society. Repeating a wrong does not make it right; it merely compounds the wrong.

The mouth, perhaps more than any other body part, is capable of doing so much good. It can bring peace and harmony, cheer and hope. But it can depress, it can heap indignity, it can wreak great havoc.

From the range of prohibited speech, insulting or degrading, we learn the seriousness of misusing our tongues. We might even dare call it tongue abuse.

Whatever it is called, it is out of bounds. If we restrict ourselves to clean, helpful, kind, caring speech, we will avoid the evil type, and in the process we will also generate much good.

## Remembering What Happened to Miriam

"Remember what the Lord your God did to Miriam..." (*Devarim* 24:9). Miriam suffered as a consequence of speaking ill of her brother, Moshe Rabbeinu. We are obliged to remember this, verbally, on a daily basis. We are also enjoined not to forget it (*Sefer Chareidim*, p. 101, no. 14). The matter is so serious that it merits both a directive to remember and a caution not to forget.

Miriam was certainly a woman of great and noble achievement, whose heroic intervention was critical to Israel's survival in Egypt. Her leadership in the Exodus, and the song she sang with the women at the Reed Sea, are further indications of the great esteem in which she was held. But we are asked to remember a lapse in an otherwise abundantly fulfilling life. Why?

The essence of the observance is "to take to heart, daily, the talk of Miriam and her punishment for it, so that one muzzles the mouth in trembling to avoid speaking ill of others" (*Sefer Chareidim*, p. 67, no. 45; see also *Sefer Chareidim*, p. 73, no. 24).

Is this a fair way to remember Miriam? And by re-calling Miriam in this seemingly negative way, are we not also guilty, on a daily basis, of speaking ill of others, in this instance Miriam? This is the very behavior the mitzvah is designed to help us avoid, yet by remember-ing Miriam we seem to be behaving in the way we are warned against.

There were many who spoke ill of Moshe Rabbeinu, as is evident from the biblical chronicle of the Jewish people during their servitude in Egypt and in their forty years of wandering in the desert. Miriam, more than oth-ers, is singled out for the remarks she made.

Although Miriam was not the only one to speak ill of Moshe Rabbeinu, and the ill she spoke was probably not as serious as other remarks, such as those uttered by Korach, she was the most respected and admired person to do so. In remembering Miriam's lapse, we essentially remember her greatness, and we are reminded that speaking ill of others is inexcusable, no matter how great the person who is doing the talking.

We must never use our lofty position within the

community to disparage others. And when our position in the community is not that lofty, we certainly have no business making negative remarks about community leaders, or anyone else.

Ultimately, if we translate Miriam's lapse into a continuing reminder to avoid disparaging talk, this is to her credit. We make Miriam the catalyst for good, which is a lovely way to remember Miriam.

## Plugging Our Ears

We have control over what we say, but do we have control over what we hear? It is safe to say that we have less control over what we hear, since words or noise can come at us suddenly, and we do not react quickly enough to block out the noise.

But consider for a moment our natural reflex when we suddenly hear a very loud noise. Even though we may be too late to block out the sound, we still instinctively put our hands over our ears to cover up the noise. We may not succeed in avoiding the noise, but we do succeed in clearly showing that we do not like it.

That reflex is the reaction we are asked to show when we hear inappropriate speech. "You shall have a shovel in addition to your weapons" (*Devarim* 23:14) is interpreted by the Talmud in a unique way.

The word used for "weapons," *azeinecha*, is remarkably similar to the Hebrew word for "your ear," *aznecha*. And the finger is smooth and bare like the stick of a shovel. Reformulated, this becomes a biblical directive to put one's finger in one's ear if one hears improper speech (*Ketubot* 5b, quoted in *Sefer Chareidim*, p. 69, no. 3).

It is recognized that the spread of gossip, the proliferation of evil talk, is predicated on a partnership between the talker and the listener. The talker obviously should not utter such words, but the listener is similarly urged not to listen. With no listeners, we have cut out the market for the talkers, and this will hopefully discourage them from spreading further gossip.

The obligation is to plug up the ears, to make it patently clear that you find this type of speech unacceptable, and that you refuse to let your ears, and your entire being, become polluted.

An additional regulation in this regard is the prohibition against believing that any evil talk about others is the truth and, even better, against listening to such conversation (*Shemot* 23:1; *Sefer Chareidim*, p. 107, no. 3).

This type of reflex can develop only if our distaste for gossip is such that we regard it as an invasive intrusion, as invasive on our equilibrium as a thunderous noise. Underlining this mitzvah fulfillment is a basic appreciation of the goodness of others, so that there is a protective barrier in our ears against any talk that diminishes them.

## Making Pledges

Making promises and giving pledges are part of life. We pledge allegiance, we pledge commitments, we pledge to honor commitments, we promise to do things, and we overemploy the well-worn goodbye refrain in the form of I'll get back to you.

It is hard to imagine that there could be anything objectionable in this, as long as the promise is kept. And pledging money is usually for good causes, charitable pursuits.

But "it is preferable to refrain from making a vow, because a vow is a stumbling block for the person — he may leave the vow unfulfilled or delay in redeeming the pledge" (*Devarim* 23:23; *Sefer Chareidim*, p. 78, no. 58), for once one has pledged to charity, unless otherwise stipulated, one should not delay in carrying out the promise (*Devarim* 23:22; *Sefer Chareidim*, pp. 134–135, no. 99).

Another reason to avoid pledges is that one expends precious energy in announcing what one will do or even in privately committing oneself to a certain undertaking. Rather than talking about doing something, it is preferable to just do it.

It is the way of the righteous to quietly, without fanfare, give the charity or do the kindness. There is no need to say — I will do this.

There are exceptions to this general principle. In times of crisis it is natural to commit oneself to noble actions. Also, at public gatherings arranged to generate support for vital endeavors, it is perfectly acceptable for someone to make a public pledge if the intent is to stimulate others, less committed, to do likewise (*Sefer Chareidim*, p. 78, no. 58).

In such exceptional instances, ego is not part of the equation. The only consideration is to alleviate a crisis or to generate more help for those in need. But, as a general rule, it is best to avoid the "I," best to keep away from making a promise and to simply keep the promise without making it.

# Behavior

## Free Will

We think of free will as necessary in a life of meaning. If everything we did were independent of our choosing, then we could neither be praised or blamed for our actions or inactions. God gave us the gift of choice, and therefore we are worthy of praise or blame, as the case may be.

The imperative to "choose life" (*Devarim* 30:19) is more than good advice. "If a prohibition or potential prohibition presents itself and the individual refrains, that person fulfills the obligation to choose life" (*Sefer Chareidim*, p. 57, no. 20). Using free will in the proper manner, transcending desire and lust and instead acting appropriately, is a sacred obligation.

However, we do not think of the exercise of proper choice as a mitzvah, as a real command. This is more than a surprise. It is a signal to change the way we tend to look at mitzvah obligations. We tend to look at mitzvot as things we do, as actions. This leads to a Judaism by reflex, or Judaism by rote, bereft of heart and soul.

Aside from misrepresenting Judaism, such a view threatens the future of Judaism. A blueprint for life that does not get to the core of our being, that does not inspire us toward meaningful human growth, is less likely to last for posterity. And the posterity it does generate is removed from the essence of the way of life it purports to represent.

The choices we make go to the very core of who we are. Choosing reflects the way we have integrated values and the way we have prioritized those values.

The fact that the act of choosing itself is a mitzvah has an important impact on our understanding of what it means to be a Godly person. So many people doubt themselves, and their religiosity, because they are enticed by society's vast array of distractions, not to mention society's vices. They think there is something fundamentally wrong with them because they wrestle with choices, with whether to succumb to their desires. The fact that choosing properly is a mitzvah fulfillment forcefully drives home the point that wrestling with choices and then making the proper choice is laudable.

Those who feel guilty because they are enticed, even though they do not succumb, now can appreciate that their wrestling and correctly choosing is actually a religious achievement. It is not a sign that something is wrong; it is a signal that there is a chance to grow.

Those who are so far removed from entrapment, who are unfazed and unaffected by the lures, may have it easier, but they do not necessarily have it better.

## Anger

The control of anger is very meritorious. That is well known. What is not that well known is that losing one's temper is actually prohibited.

Instead of exhibiting anger, we are urged to be content and at ease. Nothing, whether it is being robbed, not receiving honors, or even being insulted, should cause one to become angry (*Sefer Chareidim*, pp. 102–103, no. 17).

The Torah charge to avoid making an idol *for* oneself is also understood as a prohibition against making an idol *of* oneself (*Sefer Chareidim*, p. 66, no. 42, based on *Shemot* 34:17). How does one make an idol of oneself? When one habitually becomes angry, one's sacred soul departs and is replaced by a bad spirit, by an idolatrous alternative (*Zohar*, cited in *Sefer Chareidim*, p. 65, no. 42).

How is anger a manifestation of idolatry? There are many possible ways to understand this, but perhaps the most fundamental is that letting loose with a temperamental outburst is a capitulation to one's base urges. It is easy to get angry, much more difficult to remain in control. In getting angry, one is disobeying one's higher calling.

Often those who become angry think they will feel better for getting the hostility out of their system. That is wrong. Expressing anger reinforces the anger rather than eliminating it. That is the conclusion of recent psychological literature on anger. But the Torah has taught us this all along.

Becoming angry is a classic instance of obeying one's lower instincts rather than doing what is proper. Anger begets more anger and is unlikely to effect improved conditions, unless the improvement is rooted in fear.

In life we must always carefully weigh what we do,

why we do it, and what are the consequences. Godliness is never found in the fire of anger. Godliness, and inspiration toward betterment, are found in tranquility. Anger begets hostility; calmness begets Godliness. Anger is an internal idolatry of the self, a worship of the corrupt notion that if you feel like letting loose, do it. That is idolatrous in its essence and its implications.

There are times when we must react with anger, at injustice, for example. But we never lose our temper; we use it. There is a world of difference.

## Vengeance

Revenge is a word that has a distinct negative connotation. Yet when revenge is taken, be it by a former spouse, a jilted suitor, a cheated customer, a victimized free safety in a football game, or a beaned baseball player, we tend to nod in sympathetic understanding.

Taking revenge, paying back, or squaring accounts is widely accepted as normal behavior. But it need not be and, according to Jewish law, must not be.

Carrying out a grudge is wrong. But the prohibition is stronger. Even just harboring a grudge is explicitly prohibited (*Vayikra* 19:18).

The difference between the two is clear. In carrying out a grudge, you dispense to your adversary a taste of the medicine he dispensed to you. In harboring a grudge, you do not dispense the medicine. In fact, you may even do the opposite. You may, for example, invite the other person to an event even though you were not invited to theirs, or you may lend them an item even though such a loan had been refused to you.

But in extending the "undeserved" kindness, you make a point of demonstrating that you are not like them, that I am doing for you what you were not willing to do for me (*Sefer Chareidim*, p. 103, nos. 20–21).

It is true that it is laudable that you are not paying back in kind. Letting the hurt fester inside you and spilling it out in the process of extending the kindness betrays a way of acting and a form of thinking that are unacceptable.

If someone does something wrong, it is always appropriate, in the right time and setting, to discuss it, with a view to resolving what may be a misunderstanding. Otherwise it is best, even obligatory, simply to forget it and get on with life.

Psychologists now recognize that this is the best approach for the psyche. As far as Judaism is concerned, however, the views of psychology are not the primary consideration. What is of primary significance is that this form of behavior is prohibited. It is out of bounds and should be avoided at all costs.

We should never allow thoughts about the harm done to us to become ingrained into our consciousness. In the end, no good can come of this.

## Cruelty

We are endowed with free will to make the critical choices in life. We may not have to choose between good and evil, but we will inevitably be forced to choose between better and worse alternatives. It is not a certainty that we will choose the better alternative, because we are capable of being less than good, even cruel. Aware of the capacity for bad that exists within us, we need to fight to uproot the bad, so that the decisions we make are for the good.

One of the basic mitzvah obligations incumbent upon us is "to uproot from within ourselves the trait of cruelty" (*Devarim* 15:7; *Sefer Chareidim*, p. 104, no. 27). This mitzvah obligation is connected to the way we give charity to the poor. When giving, we should not maintain a cruel, uncaring heart even as we extend the charity. Instead we must give with compassion.

We must not allow ourselves to feel resentment about giving to the poor (*Devarim* 15:10). We need to remove from within ourselves the tendency to be stingy (*Sefer Chareidim*, p. 104, no. 28).

Ultimately all this is linked to our faith. If we believe in God and resolve, in faith, to adhere to God's word, then we rejoice in doing all that God asks of us.

One of the things God asks of us is to share with those who are not so fortunate, to give charity, to lend money to someone who needs the loan, and to do so charitably, even if repayment is jeopardized by an impending *shemittah* (sabbatical) year, which brings with it the automatic cancellation of loans (*Devarim* 15:9; *Sefer Chareidim*, p. 106, nos. 37–38). Should the loan actually be canceled out by the conclusion of the *shemittah*, the creditor is enjoined not to demand repayment of the loan (*Devarim* 15:2; *Sefer Chareidim*, p. 117, no. 1).

It is self-evident that a poor person who senses the joy of a benefactor dispensing charity will feel so much better about taking the help. But beyond that, even if the poor person never sees the gift-giver (and that is actually preferable), it is vital that the person extending the helping hand should feel good about doing good.

That is the way of faith and the way to make future giving and helping more natural and free-flowing.

Showing compassion, fostering kindness, and eliminating cruelty have their limits, though. We cannot be compassionate to everyone. There are some people who do not deserve compassion.

Consider one who deliberately misleads the public, who entices others to deviant behavior. We are told that feeling compassion for or attraction to such people is prohibited (*Devarim* 13:9; *Sefer Chareidim*, p. 105, no. 34). Based on the biblical command to give no brief to the misleader (*Devarim* 13:9), "we are warned to have no pity or compassion on those who cause others to sin or to falter" (*Sefer Chareidim*, pp. 105–106, no. 35).

Yes, there are times when we must be hard-nosed, when we must leave compassion at home and deal with evil as it needs to be dealt with, making no compromises or concessions or ill-conceived gestures of kindness.

The capacity for cruelty that we have within ourselves should thus not be entirely eliminated. We need to have it in some measure for situations that demand stern approaches, much as we would like to avoid them.

Undeserved compassion has unpleasant consequences. Whoever is compassionate to the cruel will in the end be cruel to those who are compassionate (ibid.).

Compassion that flows from within, without thought to the wisdom of extending such compassion, is less a choice and more an automatic response. Normally such a reflex is laudable, but if it is out of control, it is less than ideal.

## Crying

Good actors are able to cry for the camera even though the reason they are crying is because it is part of the script. They are not expressing real emotion; they are merely putting on a pretense that must be projected as real and genuine, like artificial flowers.

Crying seems to be an emotion that cannot be legislated if it is to be sincerely felt. Once we are told to cry, the crying is artificial. But it is possible to suggest a level of relationship with others that would translate into genuine crying.

The specific directive "and your kin, the entire

house of Israel, should lament the loss by fire" (*Vayikra* 10:6) is a command to Israel to mourn the death of two of Aharon's children, Nadav and Avihu. This is a prototype for a more general rule: whenever a worthy person passes away, we should cry over the passing (*Sefer Chareidim*, p. 68, no. 3; see also p. 76, no. 49).

If our relationship with worthy people is one of appreciation of them and their worthiness, then we will naturally feel the gravity of the loss when they pass away.

Conversely, if the death of a worthy person, of one who has bettered the community, is met with a "So what" or a less than heartfelt lament, this indicates a profound lack of appreciation for a person who is worthy.

The passing of those who are close to us, who impact on our lives, whether related or unrelated, is met with a true sense of grief, accompanied by naturally flowing tears over the loss. There are those, in contrast, who help the community, including everyone in it, even though the personal link is not that close. What these people have achieved should be appreciated, their lives celebrated — and their passing lamented.

Crying cannot be legislated, but creating the appreciative climate in which crying expresses a sincere feeling is the subject of another mitzvah that is too much of a secret.

# Attitudes

## *Thought Control*

It is complicated enough to enforce regulations that deal with outward behavior. We venture into the impossible when attempting to regulate thoughts.

Nevertheless, since it is thinking that governs behavior, it is important for the Torah to provide guidance regarding our thoughts, to head off unwelcome behavior.

Generally, based on the warning that we should not follow the whims of the heart (*Bemidbar* 15:39), we are instructed "not to contemplate committing a sin or any other wrong" (*Sefer Chareidim*, p. 105, no. 29). No one but the person contemplating the sin, and God, will know, but that is more than sufficient reason to refrain.

An additional prohibition warns against harboring lustful thoughts during the day that will have serious implications at night (*Devarim* 23:10; *Sefer Chareidim*, p. 105, no. 30). There are also restrictions against staring for lustful purposes at those who are forbidden to us in marriage or even just staring for pleasure (*Bemidbar* 15:39; *Devarim* 23:10; *Sefer Chareidim*, p. 106, nos. 1, 4).

It is degrading to stare at anyone. It is not only degrading to the person being stared at; it is also degrading to the one doing the staring. Even if the interaction remains at the level of a stare, it is objectionable because of the harm it does to others in terms of how they are viewed and because of the harm to the one harboring the wayward thoughts.

Human beings are not objects; they are people to be respected. When we diminish others by treating them as objects, we have diminished God's creation. We have distorted the essential holy nature of people.

In our minds we can convince ourselves of the truth in all this and thereby avoid the pitfalls that would lead us into a behavior pattern that must be avoided.

## Fear

A primary expression of authentic faith is that God is ever present in our consciousness. Our desire is to fulfill God's mandate for us. We tremble at the enormity of the task, but we do not live in fear. True faith is an expression rooted in love, not in fear.

Certainly, in a life permeated by faith, there is no room for fear of any mortal. The Bible exhorts us not to fear anyone (*Devarim* 7:17–18, 20:1).

There is another form of fear that must be avoided. This is the fear that rendering justice may cause bodily harm from the party receiving the short end of the judicial stick. We are not to be deterred by this (ibid. 1:17). Instead we should believe that no harm will befall us when we judge righteously (*Sefer Chareidim*, p. 105, no. 32).

This issue goes beyond the courts. There are times when one is in the minority against a majority that is up to no good. One is obliged to stand up for what is right, even when it may not be the popular thing to do (*Shemot* 23:2; *Sefer Chareidim*, p. 113, no. 47).

Faith and confidence in God must be the guide and the parameter for judgment. Faith and trust in God should obviate all fear of harm from mortals.

Admittedly this is difficult, not quite as facile as presented, but throughout history those who possessed genuine, uncompromising faith refused to yield to any man and were fearless of any mortal, no matter how powerful.

## Hope

One of the key differences between a person who is happy and a person who is depressed is in their attitude toward "tomorrow." The happy person enjoys the present and looks forward to the future. The depressed person cannot enjoy the present because that person usually sees no future and therefore no point in struggling through the present.

In a word, the depressed person is often bereft of hope, and therefore unfortunately gives up hope, gives up on life.

There is a specific directive concerning our being hopeful, not giving up even in the most challenging circumstances. "Even when we see imminent danger, we should not despair of God's compassion; rather, we should hope for God's salvation" (*Devarim* 7:17–18, 20:1; *Sefer Chareidim*, p. 105, no. 31).

This is a general formula for hope, that no matter how bad a situation we may be in, we should realize that

God can help and we should never give up.

Faith in God does not imply that we do nothing and throw everything into God's lap. It means that we should do everything we can, as partners with God, and hope that God will help us in direct relation to how much we are helping ourselves.

There is no virtue to hope when everything is in order and needs no change. Hope becomes operative when matters are off course and we yearn for divine intervention.

## Envy

Envy is pernicious. It evinces a narcissistic penchant that may get out of control, starting with a lack of satisfaction at one's own life situation and ending with upending the situation of other peoples' lives.

Take a person who has an eye for a married woman. Just harboring in one's heart the desire to marry her is prohibited (*Shemot* 20:14; *Devarim* 5:18; *Sefer Chareidim*, p. 100, nos. 2–5). This is a rare instance when a thought, as opposed to a deed, is explicitly prohibited.

The envy is bad enough. It is rendered even worse when the envious person engages in nefarious activity to separate the married woman from her husband in order to be able to marry her. This escalates the envy into active coveting, another prohibition (*Sefer Chareidim*, p. 100, nos. 2–5). The prohibition is no less serious when it is the woman who desires a married man and does whatever she can to engineer his divorcing his wife to marry her.

The envy syndrome in its entirety is strictly forbidden. This applies to anything one eyes, and to engaging in the active process of obtaining, even if by legal means, from others who had no desire to part with the coveted item.

The envy prohibition is the culminating regulation in the Ten Commandments, more literally the "Ten Utterances" or the "Ten Pronouncements." Envy betrays a lack of faith. One who profoundly believes in God would not use dubious means to upset the status quo for self-serving reasons, if for no other reason than because such activity is prohibited by God.

But it extends far beyond this. The envious person is actually questioning God's agenda, trying to undo a situation God has orchestrated. Envy is, at its root, a virulent sacrilege, a renunciation of faith, which, left unchecked, can cause massive harm.

## *Arrogance*

Arrogance is a repulsive character trait. We do not need a Torah prohibition to know that arrogance must be avoided at all costs.

It may actually be surprising to learn that something as offensive as arrogance needs to be specifically prohibited, yet this is the case (*Devarim* 8:12–14; *Sefer Chareidim*, pp. 101–102, no. 15, p. 106, no. 2).

Another manifestation of arrogance, boastfulness, is likewise prohibited. Even people whom one may excuse for being boastful, such as monarchs, must nevertheless remain humble (*Sefer Chareidim*, p. 102, no. 16).

Why is it necessary to drive home a point on an issue that is so self-evident?

The necessity is more than to render officially that which is repulsive into something that is explicitly prohibited, although that, too, is vital.

The fact that it is a prohibition emphasizes that arrogance is a grave matter, likened to idolatry, and worthy of wholesale condemnation (*Sefer Chareidim*, pp. 101–102, no. 15). Anyone who has fully integrated the essence of faith, who understands the implications of belief in God, could not possibly be arrogant. If there is arrogance, then this must be due to a glaring absence of God.

In the presence of God, how can anyone dare to be boastful or arrogant? In full faith we set God before us at all times, and we realize that whatever we achieve in life is thanks to God's blessings. In the face of these realizations we are humble.

Arrogance, aside from being socially repulsive, is also religiously impossible. God and arrogance do not mix.

## Self-righteousness

One of the most bandied about concepts in modern psychological thinking is that of self-esteem. Low self-esteem is implicated in everything from delinquency to alcoholism to drug addiction to criminal activity.

Everyone who is involved in treating the vulnerable or in teaching the young, or in managing any group, is cautioned to nurture self-esteem in those they deal with.

But self-esteem has its downside, specially when carried to an extreme, such as feeling so superior that one feels one can do no wrong. That is as bad, if not worse, than low self-esteem. Like most things in life, balance is crucial.

The balance is struck in an interesting combination of Torah prescriptions. On the one hand, we are not to ascribe anything good that happens to us as related to our being righteous (*Devarim* 9:4). The reason for this is that we should not, in the first place, think of ourselves as righteous (*Sefer Chareidim*, p. 104, no. 25); we are definitely called on to be righteous, but we are never really there. We should always be in the striving mode.

On the other hand, a person is not allowed to curse himself (*Devarim* 4:9, 15; *Sefer Chareidim*, p. 109, no. 16). We can easily understand that cursing others is prohibited. But the prohibition is strict, and actually compounded, with the cursing of oneself.

Cursing, aside from the damage it may cause to the person inflicting himself, is related to a low feeling about oneself, so low that one thinks one deserves to be cursed. If others will not do it, then the curse is self-imposed.

But such low self-esteem can only be the harbinger of bad results. Those who think of themselves as worthy of being cursed are likely to embark on ways of life that become a self-fulfilling prophecy. If a person thinks of himself as bad, he will behave badly, to prove himself correct in his skewered judgement.

It is in the middle ground, between self-righteousness and self-flagellation, that one must place oneself — good enough to do better and never so bad as to be incapable of good.

## Happiness

It is difficult to serve God when one is melancholy. It is hard to expect of someone who is despondent and sees little reason to live to be grateful to God for the seemingly useless life with which one is blessed.

On the other hand, it is likewise hard to expect of people that they be happy at all times. There are occasions in life when one is naturally happy — at one's wedding, the birth of one's children, the marriage of one's children, and even more mundane events like a job promotion or winning a lottery.

Sustained happiness is more complicated, more of a challenge to maintain through the entirety of a lifetime. It helps to have a positive and accepting attitude, but happiness is more than a matter of attitude.

There are times of mandated happiness. We are asked, for example, to rejoice on the festivals (*Devarim* 16:14). This the basis for the rule that during the entirety of the festivals, including Pesach and Sukkot, one may not deliver a mournful eulogy (*Sefer Chareidim*, p. 80, no. 11). Festivals are celebrative times (see *Sefer Chareidim*, p. 82, no. 2), when eating and drinking are prescribed and fasting is prohibited (based on *Devarim* 16:14; *Sefer Chareidim*, p. 82, no. 4).

But it would be a mistake to think that just by avoiding eulogies we have fulfilled the requirement to rejoice. Happiness is more than the absence of sadness. It is the presence of a joyous spirit, an overflow of gratitude for the life with which one is blessed and the opportunities that beckon.

Since the festivals celebrate great deliverances by God, as well as great blessings from God, the dictum that prescribes joyousness on the festivals is effectively an obligation to appreciate the good with which we are blessed by God, including the most basic good — life itself.

It is a true festival only if we apprehend the festive nature of the day and behave accordingly. The intense, constant joy of the festivals should then spill over into a more finely tuned joyous spirit that governs our every day.

There are surely times when sadness is the order of the day, but otherwise, appreciation, gratitude, satisfaction, all components of a happy spirit, should be the rule.

# Afterword

Looking back at all that has been presented in this volume, we gain a picture of Judaism that is undoubtedly startling to many. Who really thinks that among the biblical directives — the Torah obligations — are such mitzvah responsibilities as being happy, avoiding anger, crying, and maintaining hope?

And within the relatively well-known obligations, there are so many little-known nuances, primary offshoots of the mitzvot.

This book was full of surprises. But this should not be surprising. After all, since the Torah is God's teachings to us, it is to be expected that the formula for life transmitted by God to us would cover the full gamut of our lives, including actions, attitudes, thoughts, and feelings.

The myth that Judaism is only about doing, and not

about matters of the heart, is more than addressed. It is put to rest, fully and permanently. Misconceptions about Judaism are removed. Doubts about Judaism's relevance are resolved.

The great challenge now stems from the realization that it is foolhardy to see Judaism as a smorgasbord, offering a multiplicity of options from which one can pick and choose. After all, one can hardly justify ignoring such vital components of life as controlling one's temper and avoiding envy.

It is the totality of life that Judaism addresses, and the totality of life with which we must be concerned. That is both a wonderful opportunity and an enormous challenge. But as overwhelming as it is, the challenge is commensurately rewarding.

# *About the author*

Rabbi Reuven P. Bulka received his rabbinic ordination from the Rabbi Jacob Joseph Rabbinical Seminary in New York and his Ph.D. from the University of Ottawa in 1971, concentrating on the logotherapy of Viktor Frankl. He has been the rabbi of Congregation Machzikei Hadas, in Ottawa, Ontario, Canada's capital, since 1967.

He hosts the TV series *In Good Faith* (New RO) and the weekly radio call-in program *Sunday Night with Rabbi Bulka* (CFRA). He has contributed over a hundred scholarly and popular articles to various journals and is the founding editor of the *Journal of Psychology and Judaism*. He is a regular contributor to "Ask the Religion Experts" in the *Ottawa Citizen*. He chairs the RCA Publications Committee, is president of the International Rabbinic Forum of Keren HaYesod–United Israel Appeal, immediate past chair of the Rabbinic Cabinet for State of Israel Bonds, chairman of the Religious and Interreligious Affairs Committee of Canadian Jewish Congress and its national secretary, chaplain of the Dominion Command of the Royal Canadian Legion, honorary member of the board of trustees for Children's Hospital of Eastern Ontario, chairman of the Religious Advisory Committee for United Way/Centraide of Ottawa-Carleton, chairman of the Organ Donation Committee of the Kidney Foundation for Eastern Ontario, and board member of the Ottawa Regional Cancer Center Foundation.

He was married to Naomi, of blessed memory (died May 18, 2001), and is the father of Yocheved Ruth (married to Moshe Shonek), Shmuel Refael (married to Chani Hook), Rena Dvorah (married to Yehuda Levy), Eliezer Menachem (married to Haviva Yeres), and Binyomin Dovid.

## Other books
## written and edited
## by the author:

*The Wit and Wisdom of the Talmud.* Mt. Vernon, N.Y.: Peter Pauper Press, 1974. Reprinted, 1983.

Edited with Joseph Fabry and William Sahakian. *Logotherapy in Action.* New York: Jason Aronson, 1979.

Edited. *Mystics and Medics: A Comparison of Mystical and Psychotherapeutic Encounters.* New York: Human Sciences Press, 1979.

*Sex and the Talmud: Reflections on Human Relations.* Mt. Vernon, N.Y.: Peter Pauper Press, 1979.

*The Quest for Ultimate Meaning: Principles and Applications of Logotherapy.* New York: Philosophical Library, 1979.

*As a Tree by the Waters — Pirkey Avoth: Psychological and Philosophical Insights.* New York: Feldheim Publishers, 1980. Reprinted as part of Jewish Classics Series by Jason Aronson, 1993, under the title *Chapters of the Sages.*

Edited. *Holocaust Aftermath: Continuing Impact on the Generations.* New York: Human Sciences Press, 1981.

Edited with Moshe HaLevi Spero. *A Psychology-Judaism Reader.* Springfield, Ill.: Charles C. Thomas, 1982.

Edited. *Dimensions of North American Orthodox Judaism.* New York: Ktav Publishing Company, 1983.

*Torah Therapy: Reflections on the Weekly Sedra and Special Occasions.* New York: Ktav Publishing Company, 1983.

*The Coming Cataclysm: The Orthodox-Reform Rift and the Future of the Jewish People.* 2d ed. Oakville, Ontario: Mosaic Press, 1984.

*Loneliness.* Toronto: Guidance Center of University of Toronto, 1984.

*The Haggadah for Pesah.* With Translation and thematic commentary. Jerusalem: Pri Haaretz Publications, 1985.

*Jewish Marriage: A Halakhic Ethic.* Hoboken, N. J.: Ktav Publishing Company, 1986. Reprinted many times.

*The Jewish Pleasure Principle.* New York: Human Sciences Press, 1986. Reprinted in paperback, 1989. Reissued as *Judaism on Pleasure.* Northvale, N.J.: Jason Aronson, 1995.

*Individual, Family, Community: Judeo-Psychological Perspectives.* Oakville, Ontario: Mosaic Press, 1989.

*What You Thought You Knew about Judaism: 341 Common Misconceptions about Jewish Life.* Northvale, N.J.: Jason Aronson, 1989.

*Uncommon Sense for Common Problems.* Toronto: Lugus Productions, 1990.

*Critical Psychological Issues: Judaic Perspectives.* Lanham, Md.: University Press of America, 1992.

*Pesach: Its Meaning and Purpose.* New York: Rabbinical Council of America Publications Committee, 1992.

*Jewish Divorce Ethics: The Right Way to Say Goodbye.* Ogdensberg, N.Y.: Ivy League Press, 1992.

*More Torah Therapy: Further Reflections on the Weekly Sedra and Special Occasions.* Hoboken, N.J.:Ktav Publishing Company, 1993.

*More of What You Thought You Knew about Judaism: 354 Misconceptions About Jewish Life.* Northvale, N.J.: Jason Aronson, 1993.

*One Man, One Woman, One Lifetime: An Argument for Moral Tradition.* LaFayette, La.: Huntington House, 1995.

*The RCA Lifecycle Madrikh.* New York: Mesorah Publications, 1995. Reprinted, 2000.

*Sermonic Wit.* Jerusalem: Keren HaYesod, 1995.

*Tefilah V'Tikvah: Prayer and Hope.* Hoboken, N.J.: Ktav Publishing Company, 1997.

*The Shivah Visit.* Short monograph. The Rabbi Isaac N. Trainin Coordinating Council on Bikur Cholim. Jewish Board of Family & Children's Services, New York, 1998.

*An Unforgettable Hour: Congregation Machzikei Hadas Receives a Coat of Arms.* Ottawa, 1998.

*Judaism on Illness and Suffering.* Northvale, N.J.: Jason Aronson Publications, 1998.

*Answers to Questions of the Spirit.* Ottawa, Canada: Ottawa Citizen, 2000.

*Modern Folk Judaism.* Hoboken, N.J.: Ktav Publishing Company, 2001.